WAITING AND BEING

WAITING AND BEING

CREATION, FREEDOM, AND GRACE IN WESTERN THEOLOGY

JOSHUA B. DAVIS

Fortress Press
Minneapolis

WAITING AND BEING

Creation, Freedom, and Grace in Western Theology

Cover design: Alisha Lofgren

Library of Congress Cataloging-in-Publication Data

Print ISBN: 978-0-8006-9990-1

eBook ISBN: 978-1-4514-6522-8

The paper used in this publication meets the minimum requirements of American National Standard for Information Sciences — Permanence of Paper for Printed Library Materials, ANSI Z329.48-1984.

Manufactured in the U.S.A.

This book was produced using PressBooks.com, and PDF rendering was done by PrinceXML.

For Joshua Daniel Davis

CONTENTS

Acknowledgments

This work would not have been possible without the encouragement and support of far too many people to name. Many, however, are owed special thanks.

I owe a special debt of gratitude to Paul DeHart, who oversaw this work in its earliest incarnation as a dissertation. I am also indebted to Patout Burns, my first reader. Both have been exceptional models of scholarship and teaching, and their continued support was welcomed at critical moments. I also want to thank the other members of my committee, Ellen Armour and John J. Thatamanil. I am also grateful to Douglas Meeks, from whom I learned to recognize myself as a theologian for the church. The subtle impact this made for me made all the difference.

It has been a special honor that this work took its initial shape within the vibrant and creative community of scholarly dialogue that took place at Vanderbilt Graduate Department of Religion during my time there. I owe more than I could ever know or successfully recount to Travis Ables, David Dault, David Dunn, Burt Fulmer, Sean Hayden, Aaron Simmons, and Natalie Wigg-Stevenson. I am glad to have called Nate Kerr my friend. And my sincerest thanks go to Mike Gibson, my editor, who made the project possible and saw it completed.

Tim Eberhart—ever stalwart!—has been in due turns a brother, antagonist, teacher, and moral compass. The influence of his friendship permeates this work. The same is true of Dave Belcher. I believe he read and commented on every version of this work. It is better because of him. So am I.

Introduction

This study attempts to address a doctrinal problem is theology. It is no longer common for theologians to attempt to resolve specific predicaments of doctrine. Theology has recently tended instead to focus on the academic studies of figures or the relationship of theological questions to more general intellectual concerns. The working assumption of contemporary theology, at least as a specifically academic discipline, seems to be that questions of doctrinal coherence are either already largely resolved or have no important consequence for the discipline. Nevertheless, such problems remain of enormous importance for both academic theology and the life and mission of the church.

Perhaps the most salient instance of this continued incoherence is the continued division of Protestant and Catholic churches over the issues of human cooperation in redemption and the final authority in matters of doctrine and discipline. In their different ways, each of these positions is a conviction about God's grace and its relationship to the world. And, in fact, this study grows out of the conviction that these more conspicuous of the confessional differences between Catholics and Protestants are largely presenting symptoms of the more cunning wiles by which we have sought to conceal from view the persistent incoherence of our doctrines of creation and grace. It is for this reason, I believe, that recent theology has become much more attuned to this separation than in previous periods, as I will discuss in more detail in chapter 1. Yet even in those places where the problem is brought to the foreground, as with the work of Henri de Lubac and Karl Rahner, or Friedrich Schleiermacher and Karl Barth, the separation of the doctrines continues in ways that elude detection.

I first encountered this problem after initially puzzling over the discontinuity I saw between Augustine's early theology of creation and his later theology of grace. The Augustine scholar J. Patout Burns helped me to see that on these specific questions Augustine was not, in fact, the Augustine of the theologians. He was neither the monster that one half of the theological world repudiated nor the paragon of ontological participation that the other half championed. He was instead a much more complicated, honest, and passionate thinker than these caricatures allowed. Though certainly not immune to self-deception, he was the kind of thinker who relentlessly followed his convictions to their conclusions, and even abruptly and skillfully changed his mind in radical ways. He pursued and tackled the most difficult of theological problems—creatio ex nihilo, grace, sacramental validity, freedom, election—and illuminated each one.

It was for this reason that the development of Augustine's theology of grace, which led him to embrace a position so out of sync with his most fundamental convictions about creation, was so intriguing. But it was also particularly troubling, given that the theologians to whom I was most draw relied so heavily on that same doctrine of creation. But though I was determined to uncover a theological connection between the late theology of creation and the early theology of creation, I was forced to conclude that such a connection could only be made by suppressing the Augustine's most important insights into the nature of grace and the human will. I was left with an Augustine who was much less amenable to the purposes to which contemporary theologians wanted to put him but who had illuminated the complexities of the relationship between grace and creation in decisive and unavoidable ways.

On these points, my treatment of Augustine in this study is indebted to the historical work of J. Patout Burns and Robert J. O'Connell. The original inspiration for the study was a remark made by Tracy in his afterword to the collection Mystics: Presence and Aporia, which I read at the height of wrestling with Augustine. Tracy states there that additional work needs to be done on the ways that Augustine is the source for Catholic theology's nature/grace paradigm and Protestant theology's sin/grace paradigm. This study is the result of the reflection that Tracy's comment inspired.

Additionally, my close reading of Gillian Rose over the last two years, and particularly Hegel Contra Sociology, also shed light on this particular set of issues I had been exploring in the Augustinian legacy, and did so by connecting them to the wider cultural and philosophical influences on modern theology. Like Augustine, Rose too ran headlong toward the great problems of thought and confronted them with gravity and uninhibited creativity. Both were erotic thinkers, writing from a hunger that "acknowledges a lack, but knows also that it can be filled." And their positive visions developed within the striving to satisfy that yearning.

I learned from Rose to see Hegel's Absolute as special instance of the social determination of thought. Whether her reading of Hegel can finally be defended is much less important to me than the fact that I believe Rose is metaphysically right on this particular point. As she argues, Hegel's "speculative proposition" is not a theoretical expression of abstract identity, but a conceptual therapy that summons thought to recognize its empirical experience of the lack of identity between its terms. In this way, Rose diagnoses the cause of the abstractness of contemporary philosophy and social theory (and theology, by extension) as the unacknowledged influence of bourgeois property right, which surreptitiously determines our experience of the world. With Hegel, she traces the roots of bourgeois selfhood to Roman jurisprudence and notes its transposition, particularly in Kant, into epistemological categories. I have sought to deploy these claims here in a way that both illuminates the problem of the continued separation of creation and grace and identifies even the legal origins of the bourgeois self with a metaphysical confusion in Western thought about the nature of the will, a confusion that is acutely brought into relief in contemporary theology's confrontation with the separation of grace from creation. I trace the results of that confusion over chapters 1 through 4 before offering my own concluding reframing of the doctrines and their unity in chapter 5.

I set out in chapter 1 an interpretation of the problem of the unity of creation and grace as a problem of social relations. I argue that focus on the unity of creation and grace in contemporary theology is an attempt to respond to the challenges introduced by the modern division of subjectivity from nature. I argue that the different ways contemporary Catholic and Protestant theologies have responded to this division are centered on understanding subjective self-determination in either transcendental or ontological terms. The problem they are confronting is how to show the unity of constructive subjectivity with universal nature. I note that the young Dietrich Bonhoeffer is alone in contemporary theology in recognizing that reconciling the transcendental and ontological starting points for theology must be done in terms of concrete social relations. Nevertheless, his concept of unity remains abstract in a way that unwittingly repeats the separation he seeks to overcome. In the light of Bonhoeffer's insight, I turn to Hegel's critique of Kant and Fichte, which I read in the light of Rose's thesis in *Hegel contra Sociology,* to argue that the Catholic position on grace and creation seeks an immediate unity of the doctrines identity in intuition while the Protestant position conceives of grace as a critical concept that imposes unity. Both proposals fail, as Hegel and Rose point out, because they resolve they are abstractly and negatively conceived, which ultimately reinforces the separation they seek to reconcile. I develop this basic juxtaposition of Catholic intuitionism and Protestant conceptualism as the lens through which to view the continued separation of the doctrines of grace and creation—and, at least by implication, the continued division of Catholic and Protestant.

Chapter 2 looks more closely at the immediate, intuitive union of creation and grace in contemporary Catholic theology. I open the chapter by recalling the history of the development of the concept of the supernatural as it was studied by Artur Landgraf, and note that this development has largely been absent from the present theological discussions of nature and the supernatural. Landgraf claimed that the idea of the supernatural developed in medieval scholasticism specifically as a way to distinguish the gratuity of grace from the gratuity of creation. In that light, I compare the different positions of de Lubac and Rahner on the union of grace with creation and show that each position subsumes grace into creation. I argue that this subsuming is due to their failure to recognize the distinction, noted by Odon Lottin and Bernard Lonergan, that Aquinas makes between the incoherent understanding of the will as an "intellectual appetite" and his later idea of the will as a distinct faculty of self-determination.[1] Because de Lubac and Rahner both assume that knowledge of the good correlates directly to the ability to do it, they are unable to conceive of grace as standing in a critical social relation to nature and their treatments of the unity of creation and grace are consequently abstract. They preserve and reinforce the actually existing separation of grace from creation in the social relations determined by bourgeois property right.

Chapter 3 argues that Protestant theologies of grace are the development of the critical concept of grace as a social relation that is absent in the Catholic theology of metaphysical immediacy. However, the concept of the social is lost when the critical principle of grace gains ascendency. Though Luther and Calvin understood the doctrine of election as a complex proposition about the empirical union of grace and creation, orthodox Protestantism developed that union into an abstract scheme of ontological identity between history and the eternal divine decree. I analyze Schleiermacher's and Barth's innovative doctrines of election in this light, through the lens of the important commonalities Matthias Göckel identified.[2] I note that they both understand grace as a concept extrinsically imposed on the subject, which reconciles grace with reality and reveals the truth of existence to be its eternal election to fellowship with God. I argue that, as the inverse of the immediacy of Catholic grace, this concept of election is merely an abstract and negative domination of creation by grace. It collapses the social dimension of the Protestant theology of grace into a critical principle.

Chapter 4 links both of these trajectories to Augustine. Specifically, I argue that the metaphysical immediacy of the Catholic position derives from Augustine's early theology of creation, whereas the domination of the concept in Protestant theology derives from the priority Augustine gives to the social in his mature theology of grace, especially in *City of God*. The link Augustine established in his early theology of grace between God's immutability and the material goodness of creation meant that his recognition of the difference between the intellect and the will, which came increasingly into view after his letter to Simplician, would force Augustine to attempt to preserve the goodness of creation by appealing to its domination by God's eternal will. The second half of the chapter argues that Aquinas resolved Augustine's metaphysical problems with his noncompetitive understanding of human self-determination. Despite resolving these problems, Aquinas was unable to sustain Augustine's concept of grace as a social relation, which Luther would take up and develop in an explicitly critical direction. Lacking Aquinas's metaphysics of the will, however, Luther was unable to understand human self-determination as anything more than a predicate of Christ's subjectivity. I conclude the chapter by noting that these very limitations point the way forward to a complete understanding of the union of grace and creation as an actually existing social relation.

Chapter 5 turns to that task. I argue that the social dimension implicit in the doctrine of creation ex nihilo must be given greater prominence and must be more fully developed explicitly to state that creation is God's positive constitution of the being of an other. With priority given to the social dimension of creation, grace can concurrently be understood as God's faithful binding of Godself to the being of the other. The priority of otherness in both the doctrines of creation and of grace brings into relief the social dimension of the doctrines while also providing a way to sustain God's prior act of grace and election together with the affirmation of the will's self-determination. I argue that the unity happens in a material social relation, which is a cooperation with the creative power that summons the other into being and directs it to its fulfillment in loving self-bestowal. I insist that in order to resist abstractness, the thought of this union must include an awareness of its social determination. This means that the thought of this unity as a social relation will be both apophatic and dialogical. It will conceive of the social dimension of existence in terms of Simone Weil's notion of "attendance," or waiting. We truly know being insofar as we apprehend it as a directive to serve and nurture the being of the other.

Though I am critical of some of the results of their work, I wish to register my deep and abiding admiration for the work of those Catholic theologians who made a study like this possible. I have in mind specifically the Dominicans of Saulchoir, the Jesuits of Lyon-Fourvière, and the neo-Thomists who preceded and influenced them. They revived this question for twentieth-century theology and sparked a host of engagements between Protestant and Catholic theologians, the fruits of which we are only beginning to harvest. I hope that this study might be one of those fruits. Their work is a great gift to the church, and I hope that my work might merely carry theirs forward, albeit perhaps in some new directions.

I will conclude by pointing to my most important inspiration, the judicious Richard Hooker. Attentive readers will recognize that my theological commitments are unequivocally Anglican. In contrast to his image as a theologian of appeasement, the vision I have learned from Richard Hooker is of the church as a society ferociously committed to the exceedingly difficult and concrete demands of charity, unwilling to compromise the complex struggle that that commitment involves. The same erotic passion that animates Augustine and Rose is expressed in Hooker's inflexible resolve to force confrontation with the social demands of the command to love, which he refused to allow to be obscured or diluted. That vision, its demands, and my ultimate aim in writing are best stated by Hooker himself:

> Far more comfort it were for us (so small is the joy we take in these strifes) to labour under the same yoke, as men that look for the same eternal reward of their labours, to be joined with you in bands of indissoluble love and amity, to live as if our persons being many our souls were but one, rather than in much dismembered sort to spend our few and wretched days in a tedious prosecuting of wearisome contentions: the end whereof, if they have not some speedy end, will be heavy even on both sides. . . . But our trust in the Almighty is, that with us contentions are now at their highest float, and that the day will come (for what cause of despair is there?) when the passions of former enmity being allayed, we shall with ten times redoubled tokens of our unfeignedly reconciled love, shew ourselves each toward other the same which Joseph and the brethren of Joseph were at the time of their interview in Egypt. Our comfortable expectation and most thirsty desire whereof what man soever amongst you shall any way help to satisfy . . . the blessings of the God of peace, both in this world and the world to come, be upon him more than the stars of the firmament in number.[3]

Notes

1. The early position dates prior to 1270 and is reflected in *De veritate* 22.12c; *Summa contra Gentiles* 1.72.7 and 3.26.21; and *Summa theologiae* 1.82.1–4. The later position dates after 1270 and is reflected in *De malo* 6 and *Summa theologiae* 1-2.9–10.

2. Matthias Göckel, *Barth and Schleiermacher on the Doctrine of Election: A Systematic-Theological Comparison* (Oxford: Oxford University Press, 2007).

3. Richard Hooker, *The Works of That Learned and Judicious Divine, Mr. Richard Hooker: With an Account of His Life and Death, by Isaac Walton*, Arranged by the Rev. John Keble MA. 7th edition revised by the Very Rev. R.W. Church and the Rev. F. Paget (Oxford: Clarendon Press, 1888), 1:195–96.

1

The Intransigent Division

The Illusory Union of Creation and Grace in Contemporary Theology

> *Whatever one generation learns from another, it can never learn from a predecessor the genuinely human factor. In this respect, every generation begins afresh, has no task other than that of any previous generation, and comes no further, provided the latter didn't shirk its task and deceive itself.*
>
> —SØREN KIERKEGAARD, *FEAR AND TREMBLING*

My goal in this study is to bring into relief the conceptual and historical obstacles to the articulation of the coherence of the theologies of creation and grace. I believe this task is necessary because the dominant treatments of the unity of these doctrines are unwitting participants in the perpetuation of their separation. Because this continued separation is not recognized in contemporary theology and its consequences remain unheeded, an important part of my argument will be to demonstrate this incoherence through an "archaeological" analysis of the theological history that informs contemporary theologies of grace and creation. And with this archaeology, I will be clearing a path for a restatement of that unity. The challenge will be to show that the dominant paradigms we currently use to hold these doctrines together actually preserve and conceal this separation.

This implicit division of grace from creation is no merely theoretical issue. On the contrary, the continued division of these doctrines produces and reinforces division within the church and between the church and the world. As an illustration of these consequences, I have chosen to focus attention on the dominant and currently most intransigent of these divisions, the separation of Catholic and Protestant churches. I will take this division as the paradigmatic expression of our failure to think about the coherence of these theological concepts because in this one instance of ecclesial disunity we can clearly recognize the wider significance of this theological confusion. Almost thirty years ago, George Lindbeck called attention to the fact that ecumenical conversations had revealed that many of our doctrinal divisions were later recognized to be based on fundamental misunderstandings and stereotypes.[1] Since that time, where ecumenical conversations continue to advance, the trend has been to seek out and uncover these commonalities in order to minimize conflict and maximize unity. Yet substantial disagreements persist, especially on matters of ecclesial polity and jurisdiction. Even epoch-making statements such as the *Joint Declaration on Justification* both clarified previously unrecognized agreements while putting into relief their continued disagreement on the matter of human cooperation in justification.[2]

Though there is much to learn from Lindbeck's reflections on ecumenical dialogue, this study will be misunderstood if it is read as an attempt to uncover concealed agreement beneath stereotypes, or even as an attempt to better clarify the nature of continued disagreement. Instead, my quite different task is to provoke awareness and acknowledgment of shared theological mistakes. The sense of commonalty generated by Lindbeck may be due, ironically, not only to misunderstanding but also to our shared theological errors. My goal in this study is to isolate one such error regarding the unity between creation and grace and to analyze that mistake as closely as possible for the sake of moving decisively, clearly, and confidently beyond it.

The analysis in this study is archaeological and will therefore be dealing closely with history, but it is not a conventional social history or a history of ideas. I am concerned with the logical relations between historically conditioned concepts in theology, but this should not be taken to mean that I understand the historical order to be of secondary importance. Quite the contrary, as the study will make clear, I am primarily interested in showing that our current configurations of grace and creation conceal the abstract ways we continue to conceive these doctrines, an obstruction that itself occludes our attending to their worldly, historical, and material significance. Indeed, this worldly, historical, and material significance is exactly what I have in mind when I talk about the unity of grace with creation.

I have put the concrete division of Protestant and Catholic churches at the forefront of my analysis in order to hold this empirical experience constantly before the reader's mind. The temptation that I will have to combat is the one that I believe will be the most bewitching: that is, the assumption that it is the continued theoretical separation of grace from creation that causes these historical experiences of division. This is not my argument. I maintain, instead, that the theological and historical separations are mutually reinforcing expressions of an actual absence of unity in our material social relations: this social disunity is repeated and conceptually secured by way of a purely abstract unity that conceals and fortifies that social reality.

With this in mind, this chapter will lay the groundwork on which my analysis will be built, closely inspecting the important place that grace and creation occupy in contemporary theology. Recent theology turns increasingly to this question in different forms in order to make sense of the acute divisions—between freedom and necessity, nature and consciousness, phenomena and noumena—that shape our modern consciousness of the world. The significance of our failure to perceive the abstractness of our theologies of grace depends to a significant degree on understanding the intimate connection drawn in contemporary theology between the separation of grace from creation, on the one hand, and modernity's dissociation of any inherent meaning from nature, on the other.

Union with Creation: Meaning, Grace, and Revelation

Catholic Theology

Catholic theology discovered that the separation of grace from creation was a crucial concern for all modern theology. The mutual influence of neo-Thomism and modernism is responsible for bringing this insight into relief.[3] The works of Maurice Blondel, Alfred Loisy, Friedrich von Hügel, Pierre Rousselot, and Joseph Maréchal, for example, shared a commitment to demonstrating the compatibility of the Catholic philosophical and theological heritage with the modern, post-Kantian philosophical turn to the subject.[4] And each of these scholars sought to show, from within the immanent method of modernity, that a necessary yet gratuitous excess of transcendence was intrinsic to the constitution of the human subject. They believed that demonstration of this excess could reconnect modern philosophy with metaphysics, now done in a new key, and could reintegrate the transcendental subject with nature by dissolving the dualisms at the heart of the Kantian program. As Blondel put it, the modern task of Christian philosophy was to show that "a method of immanence" must exclude "a 'doctrine of immanence,'" that the affirmation of transcendence is both "necessary" to reason and "inaccessible" to it.[5]

Kant wanted to liberate human self-determination from bondage to the arbitrary necessity of the natural causal order and a political system that purported to be the immediate expression of that order.[6] Neo-Thomism and modernism gambled that the severe and sobering questions this critical philosophy put to traditional Catholic positions would not ultimately prove intolerable to them. They were confident not only that incorporation of the dynamic self-determination of the post-Kantian subject could be reunited to the objective natural order but also that doing so would enrich the Catholic tradition with a renewed relevance and apologetics. Their concern was to show that the subject's active participation in the construction of worldly meaning was not simply imposed on an otherwise meaningless nature but was intrinsic to nature. In doing so, these thinkers were attempting to remain faithful both to Vatican I's claims about natural reason and to a modern, critical philosophy. Yet, as Gerald McCool has extensively shown, a peculiarity in the history of the interpretation of Vatican I interrupted that attempt.

McCool shows that Vatican I's *Dei Filius* (*Dogmatic Constitution on Faith*), promulgated by Pius IX in 1870, was consistently read by Catholic theologians in the last few years of the nineteenth century through the lens of the encyclical *Aeterni Patris* (1879), which was issued by Leo XIII.[7] The first part of *Dei Filius* was directed against the agnosticism and atheism of modern critical philosophy and defended the rational demonstration of the existence of God by reason's natural reason alone. The second part insisted, against the rational religion of the Enlightenment, that natural reason nonetheless required supplementation by the supernatural and gratuitous knowledge of God entrusted to the teaching of the church. *Aeterni Patris*, by contrast, stipulated only that every seminarian's philosophical training would be in Thomism. Yet, when *Aeterni Patris* was read together with the critique of modern philosophy in *Dei Filius,* most theologians took these instructions as mandating Catholic antagonism to modern philosophy and its explicit replacement with Thomism.[8] Consequently, rich experiments with post-Kantian philosophy that developed in France (by, for example, de Maistre, de Bonald, Lamennais, and Bautin)[9] and Germany (by, for example, Hermes, von Drey, and Günther),[10] and which neo-Thomist and modernist theologians had continued, were quashed. In their place, neo-scholasticism became ascendant, while a manualist methodology and the required antimodernist oath demanded by the *Syllabus of Errors* eventually consolidated its strength.[11]

Strikingly, like neo-Thomism and modernism, this neo-scholasticism was also preoccupied with resisting the modern separation of meaning from nature. But where neo-Thomism and modernism insisted on showing that the critical moment in modern philosophy could serve rather than detract from the Catholic faith, neo-scholasticism wanted to inoculate Catholicism against that critical moment. Although modernism was consequently suppressed, the questions it and neo-Thomism had raised about the potential value of modern philosophy continued to influence many theologians. Because their views could no longer be advanced through direct engagement with modern philosophy, they were instead displaced onto historical and hermeneutical studies of Aquinas.[12] Rousselot, Maréchal, and Blondel, for example, were important influences on the erudite work of the Dominicans of Saulchoir (such as that of Yves Congar and Marie-Dominique Chenu) and the Jesuits of Lyon-Fourvière (including Henri de Lubac and Jean Daniélou), who successfully routed neo-scholasticism at Vatican II by specifically disputing the neo-scholastic interpretation of Aquinas and revealing the striking continuities between his doctrine and modern philosophers like Kant. Nonetheless, the fervent opposition of many Catholic theologians to modernity also made its impact.

The neo-scholastic theologian Reginald Garrigou-Lagrange was most representative of that opposition. He defended neo-scholastic doctrine against these re-readings of Aquinas and attacked the modernist residue he detected in the movement he pejoratively called *la nouvelle théologie* (the new theology). This conflict with Garrigou-Lagrange directly linked the concern to preserve nature's intrinsic meaning to the problem of the unity of grace with creation.[13] Garrigou-Lagrange understood this dispute to be a continuation of the battle against the influence of critical philosophy on Catholic theology. The point of contention was no longer the place of modern philosophy in Catholic theology but whether Aquinas in fact taught that humanity has only a single, supernatural destiny to the beatific vision. Both agreed on the necessity of preserving the inherent meaning of nature, but they disagreed about whether an intrinsic union of grace with nature, secured through an appeal to the dynamic self-determination of transcendental subjectivity, does in fact sustain that meaning.

For Garrigou-Lagrange's opponents, an intrinsic unity of grace with nature depended on the dynamic and constructive view of the modern self. Yet the anxieties about modernity that had grown up in the wake of Vatican I led many Catholic theologians who were otherwise invested in defending the intrinsic status of grace, to be uneasy forging an alliance with modern secularism and critical philosophy. Alternatively, they followed Heidegger's lead and sought to recover a fundamental ontology, which would outstrip the modern transcendental subject. The goal of this approach was to reduce the dynamic excess of human self-determination to being (*Dasein*) and to correlate the modern split of the subject from being with the separation of grace from nature. In this light, the dynamism of the subject, which secured the intrinsic unity of nature and grace, was reduced to created being rather than transcendental subjectivity.

Gustav Siewerth appears to be the originator of this argument for the ontological reduction of the transcendental subject. His *The Fate of Metaphysics from Thomas to Heidegger* adapted Heidegger's genealogical template and forged the initial connection between his argument for the philosophical forgetfulness of being, the separation of meaning from the world, and the division of grace from nature.[14] Hans Urs von Balthasar later adapted Siewerth's argument explicitly in the first volume of *The Glory of the Lord* and used it in conjunction with his polemical attack against the priority of transcendental subjectivity in modern theology.[15] Similar genealogies have appeared since, most notably those of Louis Dupré and John Milbank, which explicitly make these same connections. Ultimately, the impulse for this ontological turn lay in large part, as von Balthasar recognized, with the *ressourcement* ("return to the sources") work pioneered by those same thinkers (such as de Lubac, Congar, Daniélou, and Bouillard) who defended the legitimacy of the natural desire for the supernatural in Aquinas.[16] Because of the close association of this argument with the work of Henri de Lubac, I will use Garrigou-Lagrange's phrase, "the new theology," to designate this ontological interpretation, while using the phrase "transcendental Thomists" to refer to those theologians who seek to preserve transcendental subjectivity.[17]

Three distinct forms of Thomism, then, emerged from the milieu of the Catholic response to modern critical philosophy: neo-scholasticism, transcendental Thomism, and the new theology. For each of these schools, the preservation of the inherent connection between meaning and nature was essential, and was transposed into a debate about the right interpretation of the teaching of Thomas Aquinas on the natural desire for the supernatural. It will be helpful to look at each one of these schools of thought in turn.

Neo-scholasticism dominated the later decades of the nineteenth century and the early decades of the twentieth. It is now remembered, and not unjustly, as a reactionary and conservative force in modern Catholic theology.[18] However, its position was largely consistent with the plain sense of both *Dei Filius* and *Aeterni Patris*, which set forth straightforward opposition to critical philosophy and reasserted the objective rationality of nature and the supernatural authority of the church. It was on these bases that neo-scholasticism mounted its vigorous defense of its reading of Aquinas. The neo-scholastic response to the arguments for grace's intrinsic relation to nature was principally concerned to maintain the immediate, objective union of meaning and nature and to refuse to cede any ground to a critical, modern subjectivity.[19] Grace, like truth, neo-scholastics thought, must be objectively given in the world and not located in the subjective dynamism of the individual consciousness.[20] Furthermore, precisely because it was gratuitous and not necessary, grace could not in any way be conceived of as anticipated by nature without it also being necessary to that nature. Grace would itself be an integral aspect of the inherent meaning of the world.

As a result of this distinction of grace from nature, neo-scholasticism also maintained two distinct goals for human life: a natural and a supernatural. The natural goal was the happy harmony of life recognized even by pagan philosophy, acquired through the cultivation of the cardinal virtues (prudence, justice, temperance, and courage). Those virtues were understood to embody a rightly ordered relation to the rational law and order of nature. The second, supernatural goal was added to this order and transcended its natural capacities, not in the sense of being opposed to nature but in the sense of its elevation. This superadded gift reoriented human life through the objective grace of the church to the theological virtues (faith, hope, and charity) that are fulfilled in the beatific vision.[21]

The new theology, by contrast, reiterated the arguments of earlier neo-Thomism and modernism but cast them, according to the limitations imposed on Catholic theology after *Dei Filius* and *Aeterni Patris*, as arguments specifically about Aquinas's doctrine of grace. Before the Second Vatican Council, the label "new theology" referred to the theological challenges levied at neo-scholastics' interpretation of Aquinas; but after the council, it could be applied to the work of those thinkers who maintained an intrinsic relation of grace to nature but who, out of distaste for secularism, rejected the priority granted to modern subjectivity. For these commitments, these thinkers are rightly distinguished from transcendental Thomists.[22] The new theology maintained the transcendent excess that Maréchal, Blondel, and Rousselot uncovered in subjectivity. As Henri de Lubac put it in his early work *The Discovery of God*, repeating Maréchal (and agreeing with Rahner), God is implicitly known—or pre-thematically known—in every act of knowing as the final, complete goal of every act of understanding. But this dynamism is understood primarily as the disclosure of humanity's ontological status as creatures, which likewise serves as the bond between nature and the supernatural.[23] The focus is not with the dynamic constitution of human subjectivity but with the ontological significance—the meaning—of being a spiritual creature.

Commonly, neo-scholasticism and the new theology are perceived as enemies. It certainly is true that the new theology embarked on retrieving a positive appraisal of critical philosophy and embraced an intrinsic relation of grace to nature that neo-scholasticism opposed, but the tension between these two positions should not obscure their common anxiety about the modern secularism they took to be the inevitable consequence of transcendental subjectivity. De Lubac's arguments in *The Drama of Atheist Humanism* and his essay "The Internal Causes of the Weakening and the Disappearance of the Sense of the Sacred," for example, offer an utterly bleak diagnosis of the diseased condition of modern culture. In fact, de Lubac's major concern with neo-scholastic objectivity is that it too separates the subject from nature. His arguments in *Catholicism* and *Corpus Mysticum*, for example, are polemical attacks against the encroachment of Enlightenment rationalism and bureaucracy into the church's naturally organic coincidence of universal and particular. For de Lubac, the full routing of modernity required an account of graced nature, which alone could reunite the objective and the subjective poles of experience in a single account of creation as God's gratuitous self-expression.

Finally, transcendental Thomism also grew out of the same neo-Thomist and modernist arguments that became the new theology. However, the transcendental Thomists attributed the disorders they found in modernity not to its diseased culture but to the fact that modernity had ceased to locate the meaning and intelligibility of experience in God. Human experience was no longer implicitly understood as an aspect of God's self-communication. The turn to subjectivity was not an obstacle to these goals but an opportunity to retrieve this universal experience. Karl Rahner's *Spirit in the World*, for example, spoke of the subject's "pre-apprehension" (*Vorgriff*) of the Absolute, which constituted the subject as a tensed "hovering" (*Schwebe*) above the world from within it, a "spirit in the world."[24] Similarly, Bernard Lonergan insisted in *Verbum* that Aquinas taught that all true knowledge includes an irreducible moment of existential self-appropriation.[25]

Transcendental Thomism unites grace to nature within this dynamic activity, seeing it as intrinsically ordered to God. All experience is graced, but not all experience is directly an experience of that grace. For this reason, transcendental Thomism agrees with neo-scholasticism that grace cannot be confused with nature. Transcendental Thomists simply insist that this distinction of grace and nature is transcendental, that it is meaningful in relation to the subject and does not mark the distinction of the subject and the object. As Rahner argued, the idea of a "pure nature," a graceless experience of the world, has an important role to play as a "remainder concept" (*Restbegriff*) that ensures that God's self-communication in experience is differentiated from our experience. The transcendental subject is necessary in order to maintain this distinction, according to Rahner, which is otherwise lost in an ontological reduction.

Each of these influential schools of thought recognized that the question of the unity of God's bestowal of grace with God's act of creating is of central importance for responding to the challenge that modern, critical philosophy had posed to theology in its attack on classical metaphysics. The unity of the theologies of grace and creation became the focal point in Catholic theology for coming to terms with the loss of any sense of the intrinsic meaning of the natural world. Sharply divergent as the theologies of grace that developed from these three schools were, they shared this common concern to overcome the disjunctions that characterized the modern experience of the world. Their different emphases on the objective, subjective, or ontological status of grace are divergent ways of attempting to preserve or to reconceive the meaning of nature. The experience of opposition so characteristic of modernity raises the question of the relation of grace to creation to a particularly acute pitch.

PROTESTANT THEOLOGY

Modern Protestant theology did not propose a compelling alternative to the transcendental subject like Catholic neo-scholasticism. Protestant theology absorbed the turn to the subject almost immediately, reconfiguring Christian doctrine according to the primacy of practical rather than pure reason. This was so much the case that, by the turn of the twentieth century, Protestant theology was virtually synonymous with the transcendental analysis of either the content of subjective consciousness or the conditions of possibility for the ethical activity of subjective agents.[26]

Because Protestant theology was so rooted in subjective experience, it also had to endure a complex set of traumatic critiques levied by erstwhile theologians such as David Strauss, Ludwig Feuerbach, and Franz Overbeck that exploited its dependence on Kant's division of belief from knowledge (*Wissen*). No substantive alternatives to this dualism were to be found in Protestant theology. Catholic theology was able to reunite the subject with nature in the dynamic self-determination of the subject, but Protestant theology was constitutively invested in the dualism through its dialectical juxtaposition of sin and grace. Consequently, Protestant theology could not correlate the content of faith with reality. It could talk about the unique relation between faith and God, but it could not show how that faith could in any way amount to knowledge not reducible to the generalized content of subjective consciousness.

The first major disruption of this liberal focus on consciousness, came with the emergence of dialectical theology in response to the outbreak of World War I. Its theologians sought not to overcome the divisions but to oppose faith to knowledge, resisting all to "possess" God like an object. If we follow the standard interpretation of Barth's development, given in different ways by von Balthasar and Frei, we can see that Barth's departure from this dialectical theology and his embrace of analogy resulted from a clear recognition of the theological consequences of maintaining this sharp opposition.[27] After his insight into the actuality of God, gleaned from his meditation on Anselm, Barth's reframed his theology in such a way as to restore this connection between the content of faith and reality.[28]

Given that Barth saw this problem more clearly than his fellow dialectical theologians, it is no surprise that he, the foremost Protestant theologian of his time, was at the center of a dispute with Erich Przywara over the propriety of embracing an "analogy of being" (*analogia entis*)[29] and with Emil Brunner about the possibility of a transcendental point of contact (*Anknüpfungspunkt*) for revelation.[30] In both cases, the dispute was focused on the fact that Barth accepts the need for correspondence between human concepts (knowledge) and God's reality but wants also to continue to deny any "natural" or inherent basis for correspondence between humanity and God. Barth located the basis for that correspondence, as he argued in *The Humanity of God*, in the freedom of God alone.[31] This tack makes Barth's theology peculiar in that, in contrast to the ontological reduction of the transcendental subject that becomes characteristic of the Catholic new theology, Barth reconceives God by ontologizing transcendental subjectivity. As the absolute Subject of Being, God displaces human subjectivity and transgresses its propriety. And, in the same way that the relationship of grace to nature became the theological nucleus for the Catholic encounter with the modern separation of meaning from nature, Barth made the absolute priority of God's revelation the center of the Protestant discussion of all proper knowledge of God. By extension, this stance also made faith in that revelation the source of all worldly meaning.

The young Dietrich Bonhoeffer clearly saw the importance of Barth's recuperation of the priority of revelation, but he also recognized that the problem Barth was confronting, which was inseparable from the modern struggle with the meaningful experience of the world, was even within the

Catholic theology of their day an attempt to "overcome the difference between a transcendental and ontological starting point of theology."[32] Bonhoeffer's two dissertations, *Sanctorum Communio* and *Act and Being*, acknowledged the metaphysical status of this problem while nonetheless remaining convinced that any adequate response would supplant classical metaphysics with philosophical personalism. As a result, in contrast to the Catholic affinity for "nature," Bonhoeffer too privileges revelation as the event of disclosure through which the meaning of worldly experience is determined. Yet Bonhoeffer also recognizes that such events have a continued history in existence, which leads him to focus on the union of the transcendental subjectivity of the human agent with ontological stability.

Bonhoeffer wants to locate the site of that stability in the ethical relations that obtain ontologically in the community of the Christian church. The community, he argued, is the continued existence of Jesus in the world as God's revelation.[33] It is not in the institution of the church (*Kirche*) but in their communal relations (*Gemeinde*) that human beings are authentically acting (becoming) in such a way that difference (matter, time, multiplicity, particularity) and being (unity, form, eternity, unity, universality) are united.[34] In this way, Bonhoeffer follows his teacher Reinhold Seeberg in seeing ethical relations as the site of God's self-communication.[35] God's act and being happens in the world in a concretely ethical way that is coextensive with the loving embrace of the neighbor in the Christian assembly. The church is individuals-together existing as a collective-individual (Jesus), a collective-individual who reveals that Being is fundamentally personal and relational.

It is where this argument most succeeds that its failures are also most clearly apparent. Though Bonhoeffer rightly recognized the need to overcome the separation of the transcendental subject and being, he embraced what André Dumas called an ontology without metaphysics,[36] a personalism like that of Martin Buber, Ferdinand Schiller, Gabriel Marcel, and Edith Stein.[37] The personalist influence was likely due in part to the tradition of Ritschlian liberalism that Bonhoeffer also learned from Seeberg,[38] and his embrace of ontology was indebted to Heidegger's *Being and Time*.[39] Bonhoeffer's intent was to avoid the errors he attributed to classical metaphysics, which he was convinced could not accommodate the necessary priority of the event of revelation. Yet he also needed to respond to the important concerns about change and continuity, difference and identity that are the province of metaphysics. As a result, his ontology also showed a considerable Hegelian hue learned from Seeberg and the philosopher Eberhard Grisebach,[40] which guided Bonhoeffer's thought to social theory and sociology.[41]

From both Hegel and social theory, Bonhoeffer developed his social vision of the Christian community as the site in which the transcendental dynamism of human subjectivity is transformed from self-preservation into charitable affirmation of the other. This is a vision of the harmony of subject and being in revelation, but in such a way that the subject's essential distinction from being is preserved. The self and nature are never truly unified. Rather, in the event of revelation, which is encountered in the Christian community, the fundamental division of the self from nature is no longer antagonistic. Revelation distinguishes the social relations of the Christian community from those of the world by supplying the concept within which the fundamental separation that makes these relations possible is affirmed.

In both Barth and Bonhoeffer, we see that Protestant theology during this time, like Catholic theology, punctuated the experience of the loss of worldly meaning as a concern with the reunion of grace with creation. Rather than being conceived as a problem of the inherence of meaning in the world, however, Protestant theology interpreted this experience in terms of sin and alienation and sought to recuperate the event of God's revelation as the locus of their reconciliation. Only in the event is the sinful alienation of our "natural" social condition, our drive to self-preservation, overcome in existence.[42] This way of conceiving the reconciliation of the subject and nature must be distinguished from Catholic theologies that sought to preserve the originary coincidence of subject and nature, of meaning and world, either through an objective distinction between nature and grace or through some account of their correspondence with subjective agency. Protestant theologies recognized that the endemic split of the subject from nature renders aberrant any claim to the natural knowledge of God into a generalization of subjective self-consciousness. Consequently, revelation, not nature, must be the referent for the union of subject and nature. It cannot be in any way a natural, intrinsic capacity of the creature and can only be God's own work.

Bonhoeffer made the real advance within this network of ideas. He clarified that modern theology is in search of a starting point beyond the conflict between being (ontology) and the self (subjectivity). He also saw that this experience of contradiction requires beginning with actually existing social relations. Ultimately, Bonhoeffer's own solution remains incapable of sustaining the concrete reconciliation of subject and nature that he sought. The reasons for this failure can be expanded, and considerable light shed on the difficulties of both the Catholic and Protestant perspectives on this question, by looking in some detail at Hegel's argument against Kant and Fichte in *System of Ethical*

Life. This analysis will be the foundation for the investigations of Catholic and Protestant theologies in subsequent chapters.

ABSTRACT AND NEGATIVE UNITY

In *System of Ethical Life,* Hegel contrasts intuition and concept in a way directly related to the distinct ways that Catholic and Protestant theologies seek to unite grace and creation.[43] Intuition, for Hegel, refers to a subject's apprehension of its immediate identity with nature, whereas concepts arise from the subject's free and constructive activity in relation to nature. When intuition has priority, the subject stands in fundamental distinction from nature as equal in differentiation. But with the priority of the concept, the subject's activity as the constructive basis for apprehending the field of empirical differentiation. In fact, for the primacy of the concept, nature itself is considered the product of this subjective activity, and it is through this differentiating activity that the subject grasps itself.

When the unity of the subject and nature is conceived according to intuition, then their relation of differentiation is maintained and their parity heeded. Nevertheless, Hegel argues, this union lacks any critical concept.[44] The practical work of construction is subsumed under the immediacy of nature.[45] Concepts are operative in the perception of nature, but they are not recognized as subjective constructions. They are known only as immediate apprehensions of nature.[46] As Kant maintained, this merely intuited union of subject and nature is abstract, or "blind."[47] Lacking a concept, intuition cannot give knowledge of the union but functions only as a negative and unjustified presupposition. Because there can be no knowledge of the union, likewise there can be no material or social reality of the union. What is here conceived of as union is merely the transcendental condition of the necessary separation of subject and nature.[48]

The circumstances are reversed when unity is understood to be the effect of the practical imposition of the concept. If one begins with the manifold differentiations of nature, their unity must be derived from the imposition of a conceptual identity. The result is not the subordination of the concept to nature but the concept's domination of nature.[49] Constructive reason imposes its concepts on natural differentiation, suppressing intuition, rather than rationally deriving its concepts from it. As with intuition, the resulting unity is abstract, a purely formal criterion that is "empty" because it lacks the content provided by intuition.[50] Here, the union of subject and object is knowable, but it is negative because it results from the suppression, domination, and exclusion of natural difference.[51] And it is abstract because the concepts supplying this union are purely formal.[52]

These two abstract forms of unifying the subject and nature, according to Hegel, are social realities. In the absence of any critical relation to nature, intuition's subsumption of the concept serves to authorize existing social relations as "natural."[53] The actually existing social order is simply and uncritically presupposed to be natural. But, conversely, the unity achieved through the concept dominates and suppresses the intuitive manifold that deviates from the formal concept.[54] As a result, blind to anything outside its own practical domination, the priority of the concept fails to recognize that the content of the concept is supplied by the actually existing social relations that determine it. The concept can only be an "ought" (*Sollen*) that governs existing social relations but that cannot be actually realized within them.[55]

Consequently, both approaches understand the social mediation of the union of subject and nature only in a way that presupposes and reinforces their separation.[56] Any union of subject and nature thought in these terms can be articulated only as the transcendental condition of possibility for present social relations, or as the regulative ideal imposed on those relations. In either case, the social reality that obtains is one of perpetual division. There is no concrete, social mediation of the subject and nature. Hegel argues that this is due to the failure to affirm the content of intuition within the critical concept.[57] Because modern philosophy understands the freedom to subsist in its nonobjectal status, any modern reunion of subject and nature can be thought only as the blind subsumption of the concept under intuition or the absolutely self-determining domination of intuition by the concept.[58] But what is needed is some account of nature's determination of the free subject.[59] Nature must neither subsume subjective freedom nor be dominated by it. It must be an integral part of the exercise of that freedom, and in a way that allows it to take shape as the law of concrete social reality.[60] It is only here that the union of subject and nature can cease to be abstract and negative.

With this analysis, Hegel points not just to the social mediation of this unity but also to the unrecognized abstractness of a critical freedom grounded in a separation of the subject from nature. Hegel's point is not only that this merely abstract union of the subject and nature perpetuates their division but also that the very configuration of the subject's freedom in contrast to the world's determination of the subject is itself an expression of the actually existing social form of bourgeois property right.[61] The modern subject's consciousness of itself as free and self-determining is an illusion produced by the bourgeois notions of property that mediate its self-awareness. This bourgeois property right is the incoherent attempt to universalize, either transcendentally or ontologically, the Roman jurisprudential distinction between a person (*persona*), who as a subject of the empire (*civis*) and is invested with the legal right (*juris*) to ownership (*dominium*), and a thing (*res*), which is an objective property owned by a person.[62] Western subjectivity is nothing more than the social determination of selfhood refracted through this distinction.[63] A nonobjective "personal" knower and an objectively known "thing" are the epistemological inflections of this Roman legal definition.[64] Subjective knowledge, like the ownership of property, is possible only for free "persons," not "things."[65]

Hegel demonstrates this tranposition to epistemology by pointing to Kant's defense of private property.[66] Kant considers whether it is moral for a loaner to appropriate a borrower's deposit to increase the loaner's wealth. Applying the maxim of universalizability, Kant concludes that it is not moral, because if every loaner did so, there would be no deposits. He concludes that this would be irrational and therefore immoral because it would result in the elimination of private property because it is defined specifically as the right to exclusion and domination. But Hegel shows that there is no logical fallacy in the elimination of private property, but the consideration of its elimination cuts to the heart of the fundamental separation upon which Kant's system is built. Contrary to Kant's assumptions, what is actually irrational and therefore immoral, Hegel claims, is the attempt to universalize the right to private property because it is defined specifically as the right to exclusion and domination.[67] It is a socially guaranteed privilege to consider the "objects" under one's power as exceptions from social life. One's status as an owner and one's property are necessarily individual, and the attempt to treat this relative point of reference as the absolute results in the irrational misrecognition of the conditioned for the unconditioned. Such irrationality is immoral because it produces a universal concept of social unity that mediates only discord.[68]

Critical as Kant's philosophy allows him to be about traditional metaphysics and natural law, he remains blind to the social assumptions that inform his transcendental subjectivity. He can submit a particular action to critique within the domain of practical reason, but he cannot bring the basis of his critique itself into question. In this respect, Kant's position is no different from classical natural law in subsuming the concept by which he grasps social reality beneath the intuition of the subject's original equality-in-differentiation from nature. Yet the converse is also true, according to Hegel, in the case of Fichte, who attempts to impose the mutual respect of absolute self-determination as the law of social unity.[69] This position, too, is an unrecognized imposition of bourgeois social relations as the regulative ideal of political and economic life. Appearing as a critical position, it is only the imposition of a normative "ought" (*Sollen*) on the current construction of social reality.[70]

The prominence of nature's inherent meaning as a theological problem, which arises directly from the modern critical division of the subject from nature, becomes more clearly understandable from this perspective. But it also sheds light on why the problem of the union of creation and grace has been such a distinctively fraught, snarled muddle. The modern split between the subject and nature, founded as it is on bourgeois selfhood, has determined the parameters within which the doctrines of creation and grace are thought. Those parameters have produced the division that has fueled preoccupation with restoring the union of creation and grace, and that also preempts its success. Among both Catholic and Protestant theologies, only Bonhoeffer has come closest to identifying the issues, and yet even his resolution can be seen from Hegel's analysis to repeat the contradictions that emerge from domination of the concept.[71] A summary look at our analyses of both Catholic and Protestant theologies of grace and creation is now in order.

All three schools of Catholic theology attempt to think the unity of creation and grace through the natural union of subject and nature that marks the priority given to intuition. Though neo-scholasticism wants to eliminate the critical role of transcendental subjectivity, it does so by appealing to the knower's immediate and objective relation to nature.[72] And the new theology and transcendental Thomism appeal explicitly to the preconceptual, intuitive coincidence of the subject with nature. For all three schools, "nature" occupies the place of intuition, whereas grace does the work of the concept. As in Hegel's analysis, all three cases result in the subsumption of grace to the immediacy of nature. This content is intrinsically and subjectively linked to nature for the new theology and transcendental Thomism, whereas it is extrinsically and objectively correlated with nature in neo-scholasticism. Nevertheless, whether it is conceived in terms of dynamic subjectivity or invariable objectivity, grace is understood to be the content of a direct, preconceptual apprehension of the natural world.

Protestant theology recognizes that this account of grace is insufficiently critical. Grace cannot merely authorize natural experience and established institutional mediations. It must in some sense creatively supplement experience in order to transform what is immediately given in it. Because of this, Protestant theology, like neo-scholasticism, will insist on an extrinsic understanding of grace. However, it is a subjective rather than an objective extrinsicism, which preserves the critical dimension of grace that it takes as crucial. Protestant theology insists that grace (in the mode of revelation) be thought in terms of the imposition of the concept, which alone gives unity to the subject's originary experience of division and alienation from the world. Grace is not the meaning distilled from an inherently meaningful experience of nature but the event that imposes meaning on the otherwise empty strife and division of natural, sinful experience.

Hegel's analysis also reveals that, because of their dependence on the original separation, neither of these accounts can attain a concrete, social mediation of grace's union with creation. And it is this point that is most salient for my study, given that the problem of the unity of these doctrines does not readily appear to us as a social problem. We conceive of it only as a theoretical, academic conundrum. Yet, if this diagnosis is correct, then the fact that contemporary theology cannot think the unity of creation and grace except negatively and abstractly means that our recognition of the historical and material significance of God's self-communication in grace lies derelict. We conceive it either as an immediate and uncritical presumption that the natural and social determination of experience is grace or the perpetual disruption of natural experience by the imposition of grace as the regulative ideal of social life. Both accounts fail to grasp the historical and material significance of a genuinely social mediation of grace's transformation of nature. The remainder of this study will explore in detail, and with the insights gleaned from Hegel's analysis, the nature of this continued failure to think the union of grace with creation. The concern will be to identify the essentially social form of this union, but in such a way that simultaneously identifies the key concepts in both Catholic and Protestant theologies of grace and creation that are necessary to recover for a true union.

In pursuit of this aim, in subsequent chapters I will focus on the unity of the doctrines of creation and grace specifically, in order better to differentiate the theological problems of this unity from the delimiting parameters established by the modern split of subjectivity from nature and its attendant uncritical dependence on bourgeois social relations. Framed in strictly doctrinal terms, this question of unity is less overtly tethered to the modern preoccupation with the contrast of metaphysical (nature and the supernatural) and nonmetaphysical (revelation, justification, and election) categories, and is allowed to emerge more fully as a concern about the character of God's acts of creating, redeeming, and sanctifying and of humanity's specific place in that work. It is just here, on this matter of the coincidence of divine and human agency, that the unity of creation and grace can appear once again in a fresh way, outside of (even if coincident with) the established and debilitating parameters.

Notes

1. George Lindbeck, *The Nature of Doctrine: Religion and Theology in a Postliberal Age* (Philadelphia: Westminster, 1984), 15–19.

2. The Lutheran World Federation and the Roman Catholic Church, *Joint Declaration on the Doctrine of Justification* (Grand Rapids, MI: Eerdmans, 2000). See Veli-Matti Kärkkäinen, *One with God: Salvation as Deification and Justification* (Collegeville, MN: Liturgical, 2004), 102–8.

3. The reader should consult Gerald A. McCool, *Catholic Theology in the Nineteenth Century: The Quest for a Unitary Method* (New York: Seabury, 1977), 216–40; McCool, *From Unity to Pluralism: The Internal Evolution of Thomism* (New York: Fordham University Press, 1989), 5–38; and McCool, *The Neo-Thomists*, Marquette Studies in Philosophy (Milwaukee, WI: Marquette University Press, 1994), 25–42. For a summary of the intellecutal background and aftermath of these developments, see *Catholic Theology in the Nineteenth Century*, 1–36 and 241–67. I am using the term *neo-Thomist* in a way consistent with McCool's use, which is as a broader category than its use by some scholars. In his use, it refers to the rereadings of Aquinas in conversation with modern philosophy that developed in the late nineteenth and early twentieth centuries. He applies the term to thinkers from Maritain and Gilson to Rahner and Lonergan. I am explicitly distinguishing it from neo-scholasticism, which was the regnant Catholic theology at the turn of the twentieth century, and the *nouvelle théologie* and transcendental Thomism that derive from it.

4. McCool, *Catholic Theology in the Nineteenth Century*, 1–36 and 241–67.

5. Maurice Blondel, *The Letter on Apologetics: and History and Dogma*, trans. Alexander Dru and Illtryd Trethowan (Grand Rapids, MI: Eerdmans, 1994), 178, 160–61.

6. See Immanuel Kant, *Critique of Pure Reason*, trans. Werner S. Pluhar (Indianapolis: Hackett, 1996), Bxxx and A822/B850.

7. McCool, *Catholic Theology in the Nineteenth Century*, 216–40.

8. Ibid., 228–36.

9. See ibid., 37–58.

10. Ibid., 59–88.

11. Ibid., 228–36.

12. See Nicholas Lash, "Modernism, Aggiornomento, and the Night Battle," in *Bishops and Writers: Aspects of the Evolution of Modern English Catholicism*, ed. Adrian Hastings (Wheathampstead, UK: Clark, 1977), 51–79.

13. Here is a good place to call attention to my use of "creation and grace," "nature and grace," and "subject and nature" in this chapter. The dominant terminology in Catholic theology used to refer to this problem is "nature and grace." For reasons that will be clearer in the next chapter, I reject this way of talking, which combines the metaphysical category "nature" with the doctrinal category "grace," in favor of pairing the adjectival "natural" with "supernatural." Both "nature/grace" and "natural/supernatural" are wrestling with the relationship between these two doctrines. For this reason, I emphasize that my concern in this study is with the union of creation and grace, and I will look in detail at the Catholic way of uniting these doctrines by distinguishing the natural from the supernatural. When I refer to "nature and grace" throughout ths section, it is for continuity with the thinkers I am discussing.

14. See Gustav Siewerth, *Das Schicksal der Metaphysik von Thomas zu Heidegger*, Gesammelte Werke (Düsseldorf, Ger.: Patmos, 1987).

15. See Hans Urs von Balthasar, *Seeing the Form*, trans. Erasmo Leiva-Merikakis, vol. 1 of *The Glory of the Lord* (San Francisco: Ignatius, 1983), 393–407.

16. The approach always harbored the possiblity of moving in exactly the opposite direction from that intended by *ressourcement* thinkers, as it actually did in the case of Michel de Certeau's work (*The Mystic Fable: The Sixteenth and Seventeenth Centuries*, trans. Michael B. Smith, vol. 1 [Chicago: University of Chicago Press, 1996]), which married the method to both Lacan and Foucault. Certeau refers to *The Mystic Fable* as essentially a sequel to *Corpus Mysticum*.

17. See Gerald McCool, *Nineteenth Century Scholasticism: The Search for a Unitary Method* (New York: Fordham University Press, 1989), especially his discussion of "ontologism" at 113–28. McCool's overarching thesis regarding doctrinal pluralism (1–16, 241–67) has shaped my focus on subjectivity and ontology in my interpretation of this material. I also gratefully acknowledge Sean Hayden's influence, whose tenacious interjection of the question of subjectivity into theological conversation has proved invaluable. Despite our disagreements, that tenacity has aided my interpretation of what is at stake between these three schools.

18. Neo-scholasticism is now receiving something of a revival in the work of Reinhard Hütter, *Dust Bound for Heaven: Explorations in the Theology of Thomas Aquinas* (Grand Rapids, MI: Eerdmans, 2012); Steven A. Long, *Natura Pura: On the Recovery of Nature in the Doctrine of Grace* (New York: Fordham University Press, 2010); and Lawrence Feingold, *The Natural Desire to See God according to St. Thomas and His Interpreters* (Ave Maria, FL: Sapientia Press of Ave Maria University, 2010).

19. Bernard Lonergan called this "naive realism." See Bernard J. F. Lonergan, *Insight: A Study of Human Understanding*, ed. Frederick E. Crowe and Robert M. Doran, Collected Works of Bernard Lonergan 3 (Toronto: University of Toronto Press, 1988). He distinguishes between a naive realism (72), a dogmatic realism (192–93), and his own critical realism, which is expounded as Aquinas's own and is the thesis of the work.

20. On the objectivity of truth in opposition to (largely Kantian) subjectivity, see McCool, *Catholic Theology in the Nineteenth Century*, 1–36.

21. Representatives of this view would be French Dominicans Gardeil, Garrigou-Lagrange, and Maritain, who followed in the footsteps of the Dominican commentators Cajetan, John of St. Thomas, and Bañez. See McCool, *Neo-Thomists*, 16–95. One can also see this same emphasis on objectivity, as I have been able to ascertain, in Reinhard Hütter's understanding of the Spirit's incarnation in the practices of the church. See Hütter, *Suffering Divine Things: Theology as Church Practice* (Grand Rapids, MI: Eerdmans, 2000).

22. On this heritage, the reader should consult McCool, *From Unity to Pluralism*.

23. It is important to note that this association of the new theology with the dynamism of subjectivity is actually more prominent in Henri de Lubac, *Surnaturel: Études historiques* (Paris: Aubier, 1946), despite the common assumption to the contrary. Here his reliance on an analysis of subjectivity as the basis for the understanding of the image of God is the key to understanding his ideas. It is later, in de Lubac's *The Mystery of the Supernatural*, trans. Rosemary Sheed (New York: Herder & Herder, 1998), that the ontological register comes most fully into view, because his disagreement with Rahner's "transcendental" approach appeared to force this on him. A more detailed argument is made for this reading in chapter 2.

24. See, for example, Rahner, *Spirit in the World*, 59. On the significance of *Schwebe* for Rahner's transcendental analysis, see Patrick Burke, *Reinterpreting Rahner: A Critical Study of His Major Themes* (New York: Fordham University Press, 2002).

25. Bernard J. F. Lonergan, *Verbum: Word and Idea in Aquinas*, ed. Frederick E. Crowe and Robert M. Doran, Collected Works of Bernard Lonergan 2 (Toronto: University of Toronto Press, 1988).

26. Here is a good place to acknowledge, in anticipation of some claims in chapter 3, that the association of Protesatnt liberal theology solely with the content of subjective consciousness, and the association of this way of reconstructing theology with Friedrich Schleiermacher, is a much more complex matter than is widely recognized. Though Schleiermacher does claim that we know God only through how we are affected by God, and though he does reconfigure that notion

in terms of consciousness, it is not quite right to say that theology is simply the archetypal contents of consciousness.

27. See Hans Urs von Balthasar, *The Theology of Karl Barth: Exposition and Interpretation* (San Francisco: Ignatius, 1992), and Hans Wilhelm Frei, "The Doctrine of Revelation in the Thought of Karl Barth, 1909–1922" (PhD diss., Yale University, 1956). For an alternative view, see Bruce McCormack, *Karl Barth's Critically Realistic Dialectical Theology: Its Genesis and Development, 1909–1936* (Oxford: Oxford University Press, 1997), and his "Beyond Nonfoundational and Postmodern Readings of Barth: Critically Realistic Dialectical Theology," in *Orthodox and Modern: Studies in the Theology of Karl Barth* (Grand Rapids, MI: Baker Academic, 2008), 109–66.

28. This point will be developed in more detail in chapter 3. On the somewhat idiosyncratic use of the term *actualist* in relationship to Barth's work, which stands in contrast with the use of the same term in relationship to Aquinas, see George Hunsinger, *How to Read Karl Barth: The Shape of His Theology* (New York: Oxford University Press, 1991).

29. The definitive text is Erich Przywara, *Analogia Entis: Metaphysik* (Einsiedeln, Switz.: Johannes, 1962). The reader should also consult Przywara, *Logos: Logos, Abendland, Reich, Commercium* (Düsseldorf, Ger.: Patmos, 1964); Przywara, *In und gegen: Stellungnahmen zur Zeit* (Nuremberg, Ger.: Glock und Lutz, 1955); and Przywara, *Gott: Fünf Vorträge über das religionsphilosophische Problem*, Der Katholische Gedanke (Munich, Ger.: Oratoriums, 1926). The standard English translation of an admittedly early, and therefore limited, work is Przywara, *Polarity: A German Catholic's Interpretation of Religion*, trans. Alan Coates Bouquet (London: Oxford University Press, 1935).

30. See Emil Brunner and Karl Barth, *Natural Theology: Comprising "Nature and Grace"* (London: Centenary, 1946).

31. Karl Barth, *The Humanity of God*, trans. John Newton Thomas and Thomas Wieser (Richmond, VA: John Knox, 1960), 44.

32. Ernst Feil, *The Theology of Dietrich Bonhoeffer*, trans. Martin Rumscheidt (Philadelphia: Fortress Press, 1985), 10. The reader should note Bonhoeffer's early appreciation of and engagement with Przywara in *Act and Being: Transcendental Philosophy and Ontology in Systematic Theology*, trans. Hans-Richard Reuter, Wayne W. Floyd, and Martin Rumscheidt (Minneapolis: Fortress Press, 1996), 59–80.

33. Feil, *Theology of Dietrich Bonhoeffer*, 10.

34. Ibid.

35. Bonhoeffer, *Act and Being*; Bonhoeffer, *Sanctorum Communio: A Theological Study of the Sociology of the Church*, trans. Clifford J. Green (Minneapolis: Fortress Press, 1998).

36. André Dumas, *Dietrich Bonhoeffer: Theologian of Reality*, trans. Robert McAfee Brown (New York: Macmillan, 1971), 97–117. It is in this way, despite his proximity to Levinas, that Bonhoeffer is to be distinguished from him. Bonhoeffer remains almost strictly Heideggerian in this regard, and his reference to ethics remains personalist in orientation, in the manner of Edith Stein, and does not achieve the strong critique of ontology developed later in Levinas.

37. James C. Livingston, *Modern Christian Thought*, 2nd ed. (Upper Saddle River, NJ: Prentice-Hall, 1997), 2:114.

38. On this point, specifically in regard to Seeberg as an interpreter of Luther, the reader should consult the fine discussion of Seeberg in Sammeli Juntunen, *Der Begriff des Nichts bei Luther in den Jahren von 1510 bis 1523*, Schriften der Luther-Agricola-Gesellschaft A36 (Helsinki, Fin.: Luther-Agricola-Gesellschaft, 1996). The reader should also consult the discussion of the history of the interpretation of Luther in Antti Raunio, *Summe des christlichen Lebens: Die "Goldene Regel" als Gesetz der Liebe in der Theologie Martin Luthers von 1510–1527* (Mainz, Ger.: von Zabern, 2001), 13–52.

39. Bonhoeffer, *Act and Being*, 31, esp. n20.

40. Livingston, *Modern Christian Thought*, 114. See also Wayne Whitson Floyd, "Encounter with the Other: Immanuel Kant and G. W. F. Hegel in the Theology of Dietrich Bonhoeffer," in *Bonhoeffer's Intellectual Formation*, ed. Peter Frick (Tübingen, Ger.: Mohr Siebeck, 2008), 83–120.

41. See Floyd, "Encounter with the Other," 93–120.

42. See the discussion in ibid., 7, 16,41–46, 58, 80, 89.

43. The following discussion and interpretation of Hegel is indebted to my reading of Rose, *Hegel Contra Sociology*, 51-97.

44. G.W.F. Hegel, *The System of Ethical Life and First Philosophy of Spirit*, ed. and trans., T. M. Knox (Albany: SUNY, 1979), 116–17

45. Hegel, *System of Ethical Life*, 105–11.

46. Hegel, *System of Ethical Life*, 116–17.

47. Kant, *Critique of Pure Reason*, A51/B76. Throughout this section, I am particularly indebted to Gillian Rose's reading, which places abstract bourgeois property right at the center of Hegel's philosophy in *System of Ethical Life*, *Natural Law*, and *Philosophy of Right*. See Gillian Rose, *Hegel contra Sociology* (New York: Verso, 2009), 51–97.

48. See Rose, *Hegel Contra Sociology*, 57.

49. Hegel, *System of Ethical Life*, 129–31.

50. Kant, *Critique of Pure Reason*, A51/B76.

51. See Rose, *Hegel Contra Sociology*, 73.

52. See Rose, *Hegel Contra Sociology*, 58–59.

53. See Rose, *Hegel contra Sociology*, 94–95.

54. See Rose, *Hegel Contra Sociology*, 55–57.

55. See Rose, *Hegel Contra Sociology*, 57–59.

56. See Rose, *Hegel Contra Sociology*, 59–63.

57. Hegel, *System of Ethical Life*, 143–56. See also Rose, *Hegel Contra Sociology*, 73–84.

58. See Rose, *Hegel Contra Sociology*, 78–97.

59. Hegel, *System of Ethical Life*, 143–45. See also Rose, *Hegel Contra Sociology*, 74–77.

60. See Rose, *Hegel Contra Sociology*, 74–97.

61. See the discussion of abstract right, which opens with a discussion of property right, in G. W. F. Hegel, *Philosophy of Right*, trans. Alan White (Newburyport, MA: Focus, 2002), 40–66. See also insert Rose, *Hegel Contra Sociology*, 6–61 and 71–97.

62. See Rose, *Hegel contra Sociology*, 55–97 (especially 71), but for her most in-depth discussion see Gillian Rose, *Dialectic of Nihilism: Post-Structuralism and Law* (New York: Blackwell, 1984), 11–48. See Rose, *Hegel Contra Sociology*, 72.

63. See J. G. Fichte, *Foundations of Natural Right*, ed. Frederick Neuhouser, trans. Michael Baur (Cambridge: Cambridge University Press, 2000), 113–22 and 165–82.

64. See Rose, *Dialectic of Nihilism*, 11–48.

65. See Hegel, System of Ethical Life, 118. See Rose, *Hegel Contra Sociology*, 71-74 and 78-97.

66. See the discussion in Rose, *Hegel Contra Sociology*, 60–63.

67. Ibid., 61.

68. See Rose, *Hegel Contra Sociology*, 61.

69. See Rose, *Hegel contra Sociology*, 51–97.

70. Rose is particularly fond of calling attention to the function of the "ought" (*Sollen*) in abstract, liberal morality. See particularly *Hegel contra Sociology*, 55–63 and 83–84.

71. From the vantage of Hegel's analysis, we can see that the unity Bonhoeffer attains through this social relation remains an abstract, conceptual preservation of the originary separation of subject from nature. His community of the individual-collective does not actually attain a genuine social mediation of union. He understands the Christian community only as a social site committed to living together in a way that acknowledges the subjectivity of another and that

returns to this affirmation through forgiveness and reconciliation, a community of the "ought" (*Sollen*) in which every individual subjectivity is recognized as the limit of one's own. In other words, Bonhoeffer's Christian community is still strictly a community of bourgeois property relations. The dialectic of sin and grace, the *simul justus et peccator*, that dynamically drives Bonhoeffer's social vision for this community can thereby be seen as the internal contradiction of the attempt to understand a social community founded on demand to universalize the bourgeois right to exclude every other individual. What binds that community together will be their common adherence to the abstract and regulative ideal, which by necessity cannot be naturally realized by any human effort. It can only be received as an extrinsic, abstract determination of Christian life together.

72. See n20.

2

Nature and the Supernatural

Catholic Theologies of Creation and Grace

Nature loves to hide.

—HERACLITUS

In 1946, Henri de Lubac published a collection of several historical essays entitled *Surnaturel*. Most of the essays in the collection had been previously published elsewhere and had been available for more than twelve years by that time, the earliest published in 1930 and the last in 1934.[1] The essays investigated different aspects of the idea of the "supernatural" in patristic and medieval theology. De Lubac's concern was to demonstrate that the dominant teaching of the Catholic tradition was that reference to what lay "beyond" (*super*) nature had come over time to cease to specify God's intimate bond with creation and had come instead to mark their separation. When the essays were published together, however, the book sparked immediate controversy. It was de Lubac's concluding reflection, "Exigence divine et désir naturel" (Divine Demand and Natural Desire), which laid out his own theological interpretation of his historical work, that was responsible for igniting the controversy.[2] Garrigou-Lagrange had these ideas in mind when he coined the term *new theology* to describe the work of de Lubac and his followers.[3]

As is noted in the previous chapter, it was this controversy that has largely defined the contemporary Catholic discussion of grace and creation. De Lubac was intent on reviving what he believed was the superior holism of the patristic doctrine and demonstrating its continuation in Aquinas. Apart from a minority of objections from scholastic supporters, de Lubac's argument about the fundamental unity of grace and creation has been accepted by contemporary Catholic theology.[4] However, the origin and meaning of the term *supernatural* was never particularly illuminated by de Lubac's work, and the term continues to be confidently used among many contemporary theologians in a vague and imprecise way.[5] On these questions, the much lesser known work of the medieval historian Artur Landgraf can help to overcome the muddled use of the term.[6]

Bernard Lonergan was the first to recognize the significance of Landgraf's work to the Catholic theology of grace. Lonergan's dissertation drew on Landgraf, whom he read together with Odon Lottin's work on the will in Aquinas, to develop Aquinas's teaching on operative grace.[7] Landgraf recognized that the idea of the supernatural developed as a way of synthesizing the different points on which the synods of Carthage (412, 416, and 418 ce) and the Second Council of Orange (529 ce) had vindicated Augustine against Pelagius. Landgraf saw medieval theologians continually groping for some unity between the various doctrines—original sin, the need for grace, the vitiation of the will, and the prior operation of grace in faith, justification, and merit—that constituted the heart of the Western theology of grace.[8] The synods and councils had not proposed a specific model for holding these affirmations together, and when considered together they posed a particularly thorny set of conceptual problems. As Lonergan put it, commenting on Landgraf's work, "To know and unequivocally state the doctrine of grace is one thing; it is quite another to ask what precisely is grace, whether it is one or many, if many, what are its parts and their correlation, what is its reconciliation with liberty, what is the nature of its necessity. These speculative issues St. Augustine did not offer to treat, and it is a question without meaning to ask his position on them."[9] Augustine left these matters ambiguous because he conceived of grace as a particular dimension of God's one act of creating and sustaining,[10] and medieval theology followed his lead.[11] "The difficulty," Lonergan said, "was to explain why everything was not grace; after all, what is there that is not a free gift of God?"[12] Landgraf demonstrated that that the concept of the supernatural developed a way to resolve this set of issues, and in a way that carried a very specific meaning.

Early medieval theologians were particularly bewildered by the need to unite, on the one hand, Augustine's affirmation of the soul's intrinsic desire for God with, on the other hand, his doctrine of original sin and the vitiation of the will. Doing so meant resolving two problems. The first was how to distinguish the gratuity of grace from the gratuity of creation, the distinction that fundamentally differentiated Augustine's theology of grace from

Pelagianism.[13] The second problem was how grace, in its distinction from creation, could be understood to heal sin's corruption of creation while also perfecting the original creation and elevating creatures to a union with God they could not attain by their created powers alone. Grace had to heal, elevate, and perfect.[14]

Landgraf isolated the key moment for resolving this problem in the twelfth century, with a distinction made by Philip the Chancellor.[15] Philip adopted Aristotle's idea of "nature"[16] to distinguish a "purely natural appetite" (*appetitus pure naturalis*) from an "appetite that follows knowledge" (*appetitus sequens cognitionem*).[17] A "purely natural appetite" referred to a creature's innate striving to express the power of its being and to preserve its existence. All the natural powers of the creature are ordered to this goal and are the means by which that creature participates in the universal order of creation. Through this appetite, the creature seeks the good of its own preservation and that of universal creation. Sin disrupts this appetite, causing the creature to be "curved in upon itself" (*cor curvem in se*) and consequently to exist in a disrupted relation to the universal order.[18]

Sin's corruption of the natural appetite was derived from a failure in the "appetite that follows knowledge." Some appetites do not arise from the creature's natural operations but are aroused by an intellectual judgment that some specific object should be sought, an object that is either a means to a greater good or an end in itself.[19] When this desire is aroused by something evil, the natural desire becomes vicious and turns in on itself in an avaricious self-seeking (*cupiditas*). When this desire is elicited by something good, the creature is drawn beyond itself to acquire the virtues necessary to attain that good and an increased dispositional facility in the exercising of it (*habitus*). Exercise of virtue increases the goodness of the agent and her harmony with the universal order of creation. Exercise of vice, however, decreases the goodness of the agent and places her out of harmony with that order. In this way, sin results in the corruption of nature, whereas grace heals it by restoring the right order of natural desire and leading it to the goal that perfects it.[20]

Philip also stated that when a desire is elicited by knowledge, that desire conforms to the mode of knowledge that elicited it.[21] Knowledge of a natural good will inspire a desire to attain a natural object that is within the natural powers of the creature to realize. Knowledge of and appreciation for music, for example, may provoke the desire to learn to play the piano, which is also a desire that human beings are endowed by nature with the abilities to fulfill. Knowledge derived from God's revelation, however, inspires a desire that Philip recognized as "super-natural." What we learn of God in the gospel provokes a desire for union with God for God's sake alone, which the creature's natural powers could not acquire apart from that revelation.[22] Only God can make available a share in God's life.[23]

Lonergan drew on this historical work to show that Aquinas's doctrine of operative grace developed specifically to excise a residual Pelagianism that remained in this account. A key element in Lonergan's thesis was Aquinas's mature account of the relationship between the intellect and the will, which he had discovered from Odon Lottin, which he combined with his appreciation for the significance of Landgraf's. I will return to the importance of the will later in this chapter. Presently, it is important simply to note the origins of the context out of which the idea of the supernatural developed, the doctrinal issues it purported to resolve, and the priority of the intellect in mediating between the two orders.[24] In the two sections that follow, I will analyze the use made of this model by the two most significant Catholic theologians of grace in contemporary Catholic theology, Henri de Lubac and Karl Rahner. I will show that their contrasting accounts of grace build on this medieval understanding of the supernatural but depart from it in crucial ways that were mostly unrecognized by them and remain widely unrecognized today. I will end the chapter by showing how these departures reinforce the abstract and negative union of creation and grace discussed in chapter 1.

HENRI DE LUBAC

The longing that surges forth from this "depth" of the soul is a longing "born of a lack," and not arising from the "beginnings of possession."

—HENRI DE LUBAC, THE MYSTERY OF
THE SUPERNATURAL.[25]

Aquinas clearly taught that the intellect naturally pursues knowledge of the cause of things. And the ultimate aim of the intellect is knowledge of the cause of all things, complete understanding, which was seeing all things in God and God in all things (beatific vision). Two passages in his work make this clear. The first is taken from *Summa contra Gentiles* 3.57.4: "[E]very intellect naturally desires the vision of the divine substance, but natural desire cannot be incapable of fulfillment. Therefore, any created intellect whatever can attain to the vision of the divine substance, and the inferiority of its nature is no impediment."[26] The second is from the *Summa theologiae* 1.12.1:

> For as the ultimate beatitude of man consists in the use of his highest function, which is the operation of his intellect; if we suppose that the created intellect could never see God it would either never attain to beatitude, or its beatitude would consist in something else beside God; which is opposed to faith. For the ultimate perfection of the rational creature is to be found in that which is the principle of its being; since a thing is perfect so far as it attains to its principle. . . . For there resides in every man a natural desire to know the cause of any effect which he sees; and thence arises wonder in men. But if the intellect of the rational creature could not reach so far as the first cause of things, the natural desire would remain void. Hence it must be absolutely granted that the blessed see the essence of God.[27]

Both passages make use of the concept of "natural appetite," but Aquinas states that the natural appetite of the intellect is fulfilled only in the vision of God (*desiderium naturale videndi Deum*). Spiritual creatures are naturally capable of that beatific vision, and the vision is their spiritual perfection. An intrinsic relation exists between the intellect and God. Henri de Lubac built his arguments against neo-scholasticism around the intrinsic relation revealed in this account of the intellect.[28]

De Lubac argued that, despite its opposition to modern rationalism, neo-scholasticism had become infected with its spirit. Its separation of grace from nature was the presenting symptom of that infection. An early article, "Internal Causes of the Weakening and Disappearance of the Sacred" (1942), makes this assessment clear.[29] A particularly important passage reads as follows:

> If our people of France—and by that I do not mean only what are termed the working classes, or the masses—have lost in so large a proportion the sense of the Sacred, is it not first of all because we have not known how to maintain it in them, to protect it against other influences? Much more, is it not because we have more or less lost this sense ourselves? For the demarcation here is not absolutely to be made between "believers" and "unbelievers" in the common sense of those words. This "frightful lack of the sacred" in which [Charles] Péguy saw the mark of our modern world (at times with an excess in

expressions that is in keeping with the laws of prophetic language) also prevails within the "believing" and "practicing" world, within the ecclesiastical world as well.[30]

This pathos is a dominant characteristic of de Lubac's thought specifically, and the school of the new theology that he inspired more generally.[31] Secular modernity is interpreted to be a perverse iteration of the intellect's natural desire for God. Secularism is a cultural, political, and intellectual pursuit of God that has become unhinged from this goal and disordered. The primary culprit for this disorder is a theology that fails to maintain the sense of the sacred that arises from the intrinsic union of the natural with the supernatural.[32] It was, he wrote, the "wholly modern" notion of "a duality going so far as to be a kind of separation between nature and the supernatural" that evacuated the sacred and opened the door to modern secularism.[33] Modern thought is largely defined by the idea that the supernatural is an unnecessary, extrinsic addition to self-sufficient nature.

Affirming the Aristotelian dictum "Nature does nothing in vain," neo-scholasticism insisted that humanity must have a purely natural happiness, attainable by its own powers, which is subsequently elevated by grace to a supernatural goal.[34] But de Lubac showed that Aquinas stood with the patristic teaching that preceded him, and that the idea of a purely natural end was actually the invention of the Thomist commentators Cajetan and Suarez.[35] They, not Aquinas, were the first to argue that a natural desire for the beatific vision was impossible. They reasoned that such an idea implies that God owes grace to the creature because apart from grace its nature will be frustrated. Agreeing with these conclusions, the most that neo-scholastic theology would allow was the claim that a spiritual creature has a passive "obediential potency" (*potentia obedientialis*) for the vision that God alone can actualize. Desire for the supernatural is aroused, they argued, only because of a created transformation of the creature's natural powers.

De Lubac notes in his memoirs that his rejection of this position was inspired by Maurice Blondel, Joseph Maréchal, and Pierre Rousselot.[36] He learned from them to recognize the intellect's dynamic movement toward God, a movement Maréchal and Rousselot linked directly to the passages from Aquinas cited earlier.[37] Having read these thinkers in seminary alongside the modernists, de Lubac wanted to defend them by demonstrating the continuity of their claims with patristic teaching. The result was *Surnaturel*.

De Lubac wrote the brief eleven pages of his controversial conclusion to that work in a baroque style that evoked the paradox of human nature as he understood it, a nature which was ordered to a goal that lay infinitely beyond any finite object. The argument's substance and style were particularly exasperating to its opponents.[38] This was particularly the case because De Lubac plays with the language of obligation, stating that the human spirit "demands" (*exigence*) union with God, but in a way that it "requires" (*exigence*) grace to fulfill that demand. A spiritual nature, he says, can be nothing less than openness to transcendence, and the desire for understanding is the expression of this openness: "Before thus loving God, and in order to be capable of loving God, it [the spirit] desires."[39] This desire is not "like that of an animal for its prey"; it is "the desire for a gift," for the "free communication and gratuity of a personal Being" (483). This desire is not the tame, wistful dreaming of velleity or the possibility of a *potentia obedientialis*. Citing Nicholas of Cusa, de Lubac states that this desire for God is "the most absolute of all desires," which is "necessarily" and "absolutely" willed (490).

A particularly illuminating moment occurs when de Lubac anticipates the charge that he has violated the gratuity of grace. The "monster of exigence," he says, is simply a "phantom of the imagination," unworthy of the anxiety it provokes. As long as we understand the doctrine of creation rightly, he continues, we will also recognize that the creature has no rights before God (485). Grace is "demanded" only inasmuch as it expresses the creature's spirituality:

> If this desire demands, in the sense that we have said, to be filled, it is already Godself that is at its source, as "anonymous." Natural desire for the supernatural: it is the permanent action of God in us which created our nature, as the grace is in us as the permanent action of God which created the moral order. The order of "nature" and the order of "morality," these two orders contain every condition—the one essential and necessary, the other personal and free—proper to our attending to our supernatural end, and both are contained at the interior of the same world, of a unique world, which we can even call, although it contains some completely natural elements, a supernatural world.[40]

Fear of a natural exigence for grace arises only from an anthropocentric perspective (490, 492).[41] It sees grace only as something we demand of God, not something God demands of us. "From the point of view of God," we can claim grace as something we "require" not because it "pleases us" but because God has created us so that "we cannot not will it" (nous l'exigeons parce que nous ne pouvons pas ne pas le vouloir) (490). This is the paradox of the innate desire for God, which is "exactly the inverse of what it [exigence] was first imagined as being" (490). "[B]eatitude is service, vision is adoration, freedom is dependence, possession is ecstasy" (492).

These paradoxes did not dispel the fears of de Lubac's detractors. Fierce debate flared up in Roman Catholic journals and culminated in the issuance of *Humani Generis* in 1950, four years after *Surnaturel*'s publication.[42] Pius XII insisted in this encyclical that the gratuity of grace could not be compromised and, without explicitly mentioning de Lubac, made it clear that he was the primary target.[43] Stephen Duffy has summarized the essential question de Lubac raised as whether it was "still possible to conceive of grace as unexacted if the theologian presupposes an unconditional reference to grace, and if grace is so constitutive of historical humanity's makeup that it is unthinkable without it."[44] De Lubac wanted to show in his conclusion that the image of God in humanity orients it ineluctably to God and gives no rightful claim at all to that grace. But he did not at that time state whether this meant that grace was coextensive with creation, nor did he clarify whether intelligent natures are necessarily ordered to the supernatural.[45] De Lubac's opponents could see no way that his claims did not entail that the creature naturally possessed all that was needed to fulfill its calling.[46]

In the nineteen intervening years between the publications of *Surnaturel* (1946) and *Augustinianism and Modern Theology* and *The Mystery of the Supernatural* (1965), de Lubac refined his position on just these points.[47] Nonetheless, the differences between the proposals should not be overemphasized.[48] Although many have noted the development in de Lubac's position, its overarching continuity should be more striking in the light of *Humani Generis*. Guy Mansini's summary of de Lubac's basic theses helps considerably to bring this continuity into relief. Mansini highlights three interrelated claims that appear across de Lubac's writing on the subject.[49] The first is that the natural desire for union with God mediates between "philosophical and theological anthropology, between reason and revelation, knowledge and faith, between philosophy and theology generally."[50] The desire connects natural desire to a supernatural object but, as Mansini emphasizes, de Lubac does not think this mediation is recognizable as the desire for God from a purely philosophical perspective.[51] The second is that human beings in their actual historical existence have no end other than the vision of God.[52] This is the decisive point of the debate for de Lubac, and it is logically grounded in the first claim. De Lubac insists on the historical rather than the transcendental status of human subjectivity, and that history shows human nature to be determined by God's self-communication to union with God. Mansini's final point is that de Lubac claims that this desire for God is expressed, solely on the basis of what has been revealed in salvation history, as an absolute and unconditional orientation toward God as the proper goal of human nature.[53]

All three claims are present in de Lubac's early and late accounts. Only the third shifts after *Surnaturel* to show submission to *Humani Generis*.[54] Yet even this shift can be interpreted less as a retraction of the earlier position than as a more intense restatement of it. Close reading of de Lubac's argument in *The Mystery of the Supernatural* suggests that he thinks his error in *Surnaturel* lay with relying too heavily on a transcendental account of human subjectivity rather than on the historical encounter that summons humanity to union with God.[55] It is, he says in the later work, because the only human nature we know is one that has been historically called to union with God that the claim can be made for this singular goal.[56]

Though *Surnaturel* gives the impression of being the more extreme work through its reveling in paradox, it is the implications of the later position that are truly radical, because they are ontologically framed.[57] With that shift, de Lubac no longer articulates the union of nature with the supernatural according to the *imago Dei* alone but inscribes God's call onto the very being of humanity.[58] The argument of *Surnaturel* was phenomenological, rooted in analysis of human consciousness. *The Mystery of the Supernatural* argues for the ontological inscription of God's call on human nature as the essence of human existence.[59] The subjectivity in *Surnaturel* is now reduced to being, which carried far more radical implications than the earlier argument.[60]

De Lubac does not argue in *The Mystery of the Supernatural* that intellectual creatures have a supernatural destiny by nature. Instead, he focuses his argument on creation, stating that God creates with a twofold gratuity.[61] God is not obliged to create, but does. And God is not obliged to endow any creature with a supernatural destiny, but does.[62] The second gratuity is abstractly distinct from the first, though the two are ontologically identical in the history of the world.[63] This twofold gratuity is manifested in three moments: the creation of the world, the calling of the spiritual creature, and the offer of the means to fulfill that call.[64] All of history is the providential unfolding of this single divine act.[65] The responsibility for realizing the call lies with the free response of human beings to accept or reject God's offer.[66]

De Lubac consistently maintained throughout his work that the most appropriate way to unite the orders of creation and grace is to understand the natural human desire for God as the mediating term joining God and humanity.

His later work more clearly and consistently ties this desire to the being of historical humanity rather than the transcendental structure of consciousness. Most importantly, de Lubac believed that emphasis on concrete history would eradicate the residual rationalism that plagued even neo-scholastic theology. He hoped that by recovering the intrinsic connection of nature to the supernatural, humanity could reawaken its sense of the sacred in modern culture. This movement away from transcendental analysis of the human subject is very different from the expression of the same impulse in Karl Rahner, to whom I now turn my attention.

KARL RAHNER

God desires to communicate himself, to lavish his love. This is the first and last consideration of his actual plans, and, therefore, of his actual world.

–KARL RAHNER, "CONCERNING THE
RELATIONSHIP BETWEEN NATURE AND
GRACE"

When Karl Rahner's previously rejected dissertation, *Spirit in the World*, was published, in 1939, it marked his entrance into the same theological disputes about grace and humanity that provoked de Lubac to write the essays of *Surnaturel*. Rahner developed his ideas into a theology of revelation in *Hearers of the Word* (1941), but he did not offer any specific position on the relationship of the supernatural to nature until 1950, four years after the publication of *Surnaturel* and after the appearance of *Humani Generis* in the same year. Rahner contributed the article "Ein Weg zur Bestimmung der Verhältnisses von Natur und Gnade ("Concerning the Relationship Between Nature and Grace") to those disputes.[67] His essay showed him to be deeply sympathetic to de Lubac's position,[68] but Rahner arrived at a different conclusion regarding the value of transcendental subjectivity to this question.

Rahner's position in this essay has been consistently interpreted as a middle way between neo-scholasticism and de Lubac's new theology. Yet the relationship between these different positions is more complex than this characterization allows. Karen Kilby has put serious and important questions to von Balthasar's charge that Rahner elected to establish theology on a transcendental foundation in *Spirit in the World* and *Hearers of the Word*. She cites as evidence the striking developments in Rahner's later thought that are not entirely consistent with the earlier, as well as his own claim never to have deployed a specific theological "method."[69] Kilby's arguments are convincing, though this should not be interpreted as disparaging to the arguments of *Spirit in the World* and *Hearers of the Word*. Kilby reads Rahner's later articulation of his position as moving closer to de Lubac's. But it may be that Rahner's shift represents only a different presentation of the same key themes. A close look at Rahner's position in these works is thus in order.

Spirit in the World is a commentary on *Summa theologiae* 1.84.7. The question under consideration is whether the intellect can know anything through concepts alone, without any empirical data from the senses. Implicitly, Rahner is bringing Aquinas into conversation with German idealism and is obliquely continuing the neo-Thomist and modernist trajectories of nineteenth-century Catholic theology. Rahner's goal was to respond to Kant's strictures against knowledge of any reality beyond phenomenal experience, but in a way consistent with the modern turn to the subject.[70] He is interested in how the subject attains to knowledge of Being. Because sensual perception is receptive, he argues,[71] all knowledge begins with an experience of the material world as "other" to the active subject.[72] This fundamental receptivity to the world's otherness, he argues, is what Aquinas means by "conversion to the phantasm." All knowledge of the world begins with self-abandonment, a dynamic summons away-from-self-with-the-other (*Weg-von-Sich-beim-andern-Sein*).[73] Beckoned from ourselves and mixed up with the world, we also look back at ourselves, return to ourselves, and recognize ourselves as knowing participants in the world. Knowledge of both ourselves (as knowers) and the world (as known) is a real possibility.[74] We know ourselves as part of the world we know, and we know the world as the setting for our knowing.

Rahner also gives a Heideggerian gloss to the passage from the *Summa*.[75] He interprets the intellect's drive to know as wonder about the significance of existence.[76] Questions arise in response to the subject's a priori self-abandonment, and these questions in turn press her more deeply into the world of experience. Being and knowing converge in this way, says Rahner, in the moment of abstraction. A subject represents the world to herself through the phantasm and in that moment simultaneously encounters the world to which her subjectivity is abandoned. This convergence occurs in the unique experience of herself as a knower, an experience in which her difference from the world is recognized and affirmed in a unifying apprehension.[77] This difference-in-identity discloses that the subject is co-originary with nature, of knowing with being. The transcendental separation of the two also includes the transcendental recognition of their unity. It is in this way that Rahner conceives of all knowledge to begin with an a priori self-transcendence, a selfhood that he calls a "tensed" "hovering" (*Schwebe*) between matter and spirit, a "spirit in the world."[78] And it is the difference of knowing and being within their union that is the basis for what Rahner calls the "preapprehension of Being" (*Vorgriff auf esse*).[79]

This preapprehension is essential to Rahner's treatment of nature's intrinsic relation to the supernatural. Because it arises from the a priori self-abandonment to the world, knowing seeks to apprehend not only creatures but also Absolute Being.[80] The summons of finite, contingent, and relative beings is ultimately a preapprehension of the Absolute Being that sustains them. The desire to know finite beings is also the desire to know Absolute Being. There could be no purely finite object adequate to this desire to understand. As Rahner notes, the neo-scholastic reference to "pure nature" could be possible only on the condition that a knower's desire for understanding is sated by the self-presence she attains in knowing the world.[81] Yet, given that the desire for understanding deepens and expands with every moment of knowing, Rahner concludes that satisfaction with merely finite objects cannot be enough. Against Kant, rational knowledge cannot be restricted to phenomenal objects, and against Heidegger, this means that the difference between beings and Being does not occur only in *Dasein*.[82] Before a self knows itself, the world has called it outside itself in a way that anticipates the Absolute it yearns to receive. Rahner agrees with de Lubac on this point, that humanity is constituted as pure receptivity to Being's self-communication.[83]

Nonetheless, in his essays on grace, Rahner argues that an account of grace like de Lubac's could not finally preserve the gratuity of grace. Though human experience discloses an ineluctable drive toward God, grace would not be adequately conceived in de Lubac's terms.[84] The claim that God's call is ontologically constitutive of human nature results in the literal conflation of grace with nature.[85] Instead, Rahner retains a transcendental differentiation of grace from creation that is a reiteration of his way of conceiving the unity of thought and being. He argues that all subjective experience is God's implicit self-communication, but it is received as grace only when this truth is made explicit. This is a distinction that is not possible to maintain if the call of grace is immediately and ontologically correlated with creation. Rahner is clear that there is no human experience that is "pure," or without God's self-communication. But he insists that the idea of this "pure nature" is vital as a "remainder concept" (*Restbegriff*) that preserves the differentiation of grace from creation and sustains the integrity of both.[86] Consequently, Rahner accepts neither de Lubac's early emphasis on the *imago Dei* nor his later ontological reduction.

Importantly, Rahner's position demands the repudiation of the role given to habitual grace in scholastic theology. Habitual grace referred to an accidental and created transformation of the creature prior to her reception of an uncreated share in the divine life.[87] Though Rahner wanted to retain the distinction between grace and creation, he also wanted to understand natural experience as an implicit expression of God's uncreated self-communication. God's uncreated self-communication meant no created transformation of humanity was required in order to receive Godself. The creature itself simply was God's self-communication. All that is required is that the Holy Spirit's uncreated presence to all life be expressed and made an explicit aspect of humanity's experience of reality. Rahner first mounts his case against the scholastic tradition in the essay "Zur scholastischen Begrifflichkeit der ungeschaffenen Gnade" ("Some Implications of the Scholastic Concept of Uncreated Grace"), claiming first that it is contradicted by the biblical witness.[88] In Acts and in Paul's letters, the uncreated share in God's life through the Holy Spirit is shown to precede any alteration of human life. But, Rahner continues, because grace is simply God's self-bestowal in creatures, there is no need to speak of a change prior to the gift's reception. Even the grace of that transformation would be God's self-communication and would precede and provoke any subsequent transformation.

Rahner insists on a distinction between the ontological qualities of human beings and their existential experience, which significantly differentiates this implicit experience of God from de Lubac's.[89] Rahner uses Heidegger's categories to conceive of God's presence in grace as an integral but nonessential determination of human being, which he calls a "supernatural existential" (*das übernaturliche Existential*.)[90] Though grace is always communicated with all human experience, it is not an ontological (or essential) aspect of humanity.[91] Instead, Rahner argues, we must speak of God's uncreated self-expression in human experience as a "quasi-formal cause" of human nature.[92] In some integral sense, God's self-giving is bound up with what makes humans human, while Godself is not in any way a necessary aspect of humanity. It being an ambiguous and imprecise concept, Rahner never gave it more precise articulation.

Rahner maintained that grace is united with creation in the transcendental structure of human experience. Consciousness is an experience of both the world and God's self-communication in the world. He insists that this transcendental analysis of consciousness allows for the theoretical differentiation of grace from creation, even as the two are inseparably bound to one another in practical experience. This is the consistent theme of all Rahner's work on grace. Like de Lubac, Rahner hoped that by recovering the intrinsic connection of nature to the supernatural, humanity could reawaken its sense of the sacred in modern culture. For Rahner, however, such a recovery involved not resistance to modern culture but demonstration of the intrinsic experience of God included in the modern experience of subjectivity. This way of sustaining the modern subject differentiated Rahner's approach from de Lubac's, with whom he otherwise shared a great deal.

A Natural Union: Intuition, Theory, and Practice

De Lubac and Rahner differ in their assessments of the final value of transcendental analysis. De Lubac's position developed from a transcendental analysis of the paradoxical constitution of human subjectivity as the *imago Dei* to a more expressly theological articulation of the ontological status of God's call as establishing human nature. The later work raises the stakes of the argument by conceiving the earlier dynamism of subjectivity in explicitly ontological terms. That reduction of the subject to being allows de Lubac to respond to the charge that he compromises the gratuity of grace by appealing to a theoretical differentiation of a twofold gratuity in God's ontological constitution of the world. By contrast, Rahner insists on the irreducible importance of the transcendental distinction of grace from creation in human experience, which repeats the transcendental differentiation of the subject from being. God's self-communication is included in every human experience and in an important sense is part of what makes humanity human, but this implicit experience of God is existentially actual, not ontologically defining.[93] Like de Lubac, in Rahner God's gift of experience and God's self-communication are differentiated aspects of a single divine action of creating. By linking the desire directly to the doctrine of creation, de Lubac makes the desire for God an ontological determination of the creature. For Rahner, what is concretely actual is the natural desire for God in all experience.

Without a transcendental distinction, de Lubac cannot sufficiently distinguish the orders of creation and grace. He has no way to affirm what Rahner refers to as the unexactedness of grace.[94] De Lubac makes only a logical distinction creating and bestowing a supernatural end. Both his early and late work argues that a theocentric understanding of creation would rightly frame the creature's desire for God as obligation to God and not God's obligation to humanity.[95] But in the later works, this distinction is tied directly to a secondary gratuity that ontologically inscribes the summons in human nature. In this light, it is difficult to see how Rahner's early assessment of de Lubac—namely, that he de facto collapsed grace into creation—is wrong, especially in light of de Lubac's later defense of himself in *The Mystery of the Supernatural* and his incorporation there of an "elevation" of humanity in the providential distribution of grace within time.[96] Rahner elected to resolve the problem he saw in de Lubac's account by preserving the distinction between grace and creation within the existential structures of transcendental subjectivity. Rahner does not reject the fact of humanity's intrinsic experience of grace, only the ontological reduction of that experience.

These real differences between these positions, however, bring surprising commonalities into relief. As noted in the previous chapter, it is characteristic of the Catholic position to conceive the unity of grace with creation according to the preconceptual harmony of subject and object in intuition. This priority of intuition is clearly reflected in each account. For de Lubac, the ontological union of grace with creation is thought in terms of an immediate, originary equality between creation and grace. In the early position, it is this immediate equality that gives rise to the paradoxical relation between creation and grace. In the mature position, however, he makes clear that the gratuity of creation and the gratuity of the calls are distinct but coincident aspects of created being. It is true that the summons to union with God, the offer of grace in salvation history, is distinct from the originary call. All three moments—creation, call, and offer—make up one divine act, which is ontologically singular but conceptually distinguishable. With Rahner, by contrast, both the union and differentiation of grace and creation remain in experience. He does not speculate about the nature of their preconceptual unity, which is the mystery disclosed in all conscious experience. Nevertheless, both maintain a primary coincidence of grace and creation in which the two are coextensive and equal in an originary, created differentiation.

De Lubac's reduction of subjectivity to being in the theology of creation situates the origin of the desire for God on an ontological ground, which identifies this desire with the human essence. Rahner explicitly refuses to consider the natural desire for God an essential characteristic of human being, emphasizing instead its existential dimension. Rahner's dependence on the transcendental allows creation to be conceived as God's self-communication in experience and grace as the quasi-form of that act by which God gives Godself to the world.[97]

Rahner's proposal does have very specific ontological consequences for the union of knowing and being.[98] Lubac's reduction of subjectivity to being in the theology of creation situates the origin of the desire for God on ontological ground, which identifies this desire with the human essence. Knowledge in Rahner's treatment of subjective dynamism occurs when the self returns to itself from within its abandonment to the phantasm. What the subject apprehends in this return is the simultaneity of her self-presence and her identity with the world. Both are known as common participants in Being, and this knowing intensifies, deepens her participation in Absolute Being. The goal of all knowing is to exist at the highest intensity through immersion in the fullness of Absolute Being. Intellectual knowing is the medium in which the union of grace with creation is apprehended and realized. Knowing is the activity in which created existence deepens and intensifies its existence.[99] Likewise, the same link is consistently made throughout de Lubac's work. In *Surnaturel*, de Lubac playfully invokes the double entendre of the French *esprit*, equating intelligence with spirit.[100] And in *The Mystery of the Supernatural*, de Lubac claims that patristic and high-medieval doctrine understands the restlessness of the intellect to be the essence of a spiritual being with a supernatural destiny.

As a result of this strong emphasis on knowing, both de Lubac and Rahner associate the dynamic desire of an intellectual creature with its free self-determination. The desire of the intellect that drives it to reach out for God is the wellspring of human freedom. De Lubac, for example, consistently correlates the natural desire for God with the fundamental identity of intellect and will. In *Surnaturel*, he states that the human desire for God is the confluence of necessity and morality, and he repeats this in *The Mystery of the Supernatural*.[101] His study *Pic de la Mirandole* makes this more explicit by stating that the ontological essence of freedom is expressed in a desire that precedes the division of the intellect and will and is differently manifested in each.[102] In other instances, de Lubac conflates this desire with the will in a voluntarist fashion. He says that the will wills God as its final end because it "cannot not will it."[103] This necessary willing of the desire is the basis of de Lubac's refusal to allow the desire for God to be minimized as a velleity. Because the desire is ontologically determinative, the creature is not simply wistfully dreaming about union with God but is actually willing that goal, consciously or unconsciously.

Rahner's position is similar, though more conceptually precise.[104] Keeping with his refusal to conflate the desire for God and human nature, Rahner distinguishes between the dynamism of human subjectivity and the supernatural desire. Subjective self-determination is an ontological rather than an existential determination of humanity.[105] This freedom is constitutive of human being and, as such, cannot be vitiated by original sin.[106] Freedom is a capacity to determine the positive or negative relation one has to the ground and goal of existence.[107] The power for this self-determination is internal to the pursuit of knowledge that opens out onto all Being.[108]

In their different ways, both theologians are retrieving a Platonic account of desire, the intellect, and the will as the basis for their accounts of the unity of grace and creation. Each understand the will as an expression of the primordial desire (*eros*) of human beings for union with Being.[109] Used in this sense, free self-determination is less about choice and more about the power to realize this desire. Given that both thinkers equate this desire with an immediate, ontological freedom, the intellect is the decisive factor in directing desire toward its goal. Knowledge of the aim of desire is both necessary and sufficient conditino for willing its actualization. With no clear distinction between desire, intellect, and will, any object that is known to be good can be willed. A subjective agent is presumed to be free to determine itself to any known and desired good.

By appealing to a preconceptual unity that subsumes the concept (grace) to intuition (nature) as the basis for their union, both theologians are unable to preserve the original rationale for the idea of the supernatural. They further confound the reason for insisting on a transformation of the human person prior to the production of a supernatural act. That reason is not that transcendence is somehow alien to nature, as both theologians seem to assume, but that nature cannot supply all that is needed effectively to will a supernatural end. The problem the concept of the supernatural was formulated to resolve was not just that the goal is distinct from the nature but that the agent cannot naturally will the end at all without divine assistance. Both thinkers have developed ingenious positions that only occlude the heart of the problem their work sets out to resolve. In order to see the consequences of this confusion, I will need to return to the history of the development of the supernatural discussed in the first section of this chapter and show its intimate connection with the notion of the will.

THE NATURE OF THE WILL AND ITS TRANSFORMATION

De Lubac was just mixed up on the point.
—BERNARD LONERGAN,
PHENOMENOLOGY AND LOGIC[110]

In the theology of grace, the concept of the supernatural supplied a way of differentiating the gratuity of creation from the gratuity of grace while also isolating about the essential goodness of humanity that sin corrupts and grace transforms. Grace was distinguished from creation in medieval theology as a specifically supernatural rather than natural reality. It is given in addition to a creature's natural powers of operation, and in a way that not only heals (*sanans*) those powers but elevates (*elevans*) them to an act beyond those natural powers alone. It is this meaning of the supernatural that is confused in both de Lubac and Rahner.

It is important to underscore that this role for the concept of the supernatural is conceptually distinct from the idea, which de Lubac and Rahner rightly recover, of the singular destiny of human beings to a supernatural goal. For neither thinker is there any finite, natural good sufficient to slake human desire. And in neither thinker is there any hint that, apart from the actual appearance of Christ the Mediator, this destiny could be attained by natural human enterprise. Nevertheless, both theologians confound and disavow the concept's original meaning by talking about "nature's" coincidence with the "supernatural." De Lubac does this by describing the originary inscription of a supernatural goal on human nature in creation, and Rahner does it through the concept of the supernatural existential, which makes uncreated grace an intrinsic component of natural human experience.

Unwittingly, in doing so, both have only succeeded in returning theology to the conceptual confusions of the early medieval period, which preceded the development of the idea of the supernatural, in which there was no clear distinction of grace from creation. There is no sense in which this meaning of the supernatural can obtain within a natural order of creation or human experience that is preconceptually "graced" because the concept can have no meaningful significance in such terms. Whether this difference is conceived as the "naturalization of the supernatural" or the "supernaturalization of nature,"[111] the result is simply the confusion of the supernatural with the natural. Indeed, this is largely the point both de Lubac and Rahner argue, that de Lubac makes against Rahner's hypothetical "pure nature" in *The Mystery of the Supernatural*.

The confusion arises because both theologians assume that once the intrinsic bond between nature and the supernatural is is established, the correct conclusion to draw is that nature is graced. Yet the idea of the supernatural developed specifically in order to differentiate grace from creation by way of appeal to what is innately "natural" to the creature in distinction from what it supernaturally receives from God alone. A nature that is graced simply means nature is operating super-naturally. If this grace is a priori, then the category of the supernatural has no meaning. The use of it confines its meaning to a description of the character of human destiny, in excess of every finite good. But it no longer specifies grace's distinction from nature or marks a specific elevation of natural human powers.

Beyond the desire to draw grace into more intimate connection with creation, de Lubac and Rahner's confusion of the meaning of the supernatural is linked to their understanding of the faculty of the human will as the desire elicited by the intellectual determination of a good object. It was Bernard Lonergan who saw the importance of Aquinas's evolving conception of the will in relation to the idea of the supernatural. In his dissertation on the development of Aquinas's doctrine of operative grace, Lonergan connected Landgraf's historical work on the supernatural to Odon Lottin's recognition of a monumental shift in Aquinas's account of the will's relationship to the intellect between the *Prima Pars* and the *Prima secundae*.[112] By drawing these works together, Lonergan was able to retrieve Aquinas's account of the harmony of grace and freedom from a series of late-scholastic confusions, and especially those of the *de Auxiilis* controversy. He claimed that Aquinas's encounter with Parisian Averröism showed him the need for an account of the will that did not require the will to be determined by the intellect or to compromise its absolute dependence on God in the exercise of self-determination.[113] Lonergan argued that Aquinas adopted Philip the Chancellor's distinction between natural and acquired appetites and rejected Aristotle's assertion that the will is a purely passive potency determined solely by the intellect.[114] The result was the first unambiguous designation of the will as a distinct faculty of the soul, which allowed Aquinas to resolve the apparent conflict that medieval theologians had continually encountered between the priority of God's action in grace and the human capacity for self-determination.

Odon Lottin was the first to recognize the important difference between Aquinas's account of the causal relationship of the intellect and will in the *Prima secundae* and had recognized that Aquinas' early account of the will made the intellect the final cause of the will's action, which conceived the will as an essentially passive potency. Willing was an "intellectual appetite" in which the intellect apprehended a particular object as good, determined it as an object of desire, and actualized the will's action to attain it. The unintended result was that sin was understood to arise from intellectual error, equating evil with being wrong and the good with being right.[115] Additionally, the notion of the intellectual appetite implicitly located the ground of human freedom in the intellect rather than in the will. The intellect determined the will's action, and the will's act followed necessarily from the intellect's judgment.[116]

Lottin recognized that the ninth question of the *Prima secundae* changes this relationship. In the answer to this question, Aquinas makes that the intellect the formal rather than final cause of the will's action. The will's first act (*quantum ad exercitium*), according to Aquinas, is caused not by the intellect's judgment but by God alone, the universal good and the final cause of the will's operation. The intellect merely specifies (*quantum ad specificationem*) the form of the will's activity, with an already active will free to accept or reject the object presented by the intellect.[117] On this basis, the will is no longer a merely passive power and sin is not solely a matter of intellectual error (right and wrong) but of the will's rectitude, which affects its capacity for good or evil action. Consequently, human freedom is seated in the will's originary activity.

By contrast, when freedom is seated in the intellect, the assumption is not only that sin is primarily about being wrong as opposed to failing to be good but also that the will is capable of performing the good action that corresponds to the attainment of the intellect's judgment about a right object. The assumption, in other words, is that knowledge of the good is sufficient for its performance, which must be the case if the will's action is merely the effect of the intellect's final causality.[118] To know the good that is the ultimate object of human desire is consequently to be able to will that object.[119]

The earlier work relied on a theology of grace that was Pelagian. [120] His new concept of the will's activity allowed him to say how a right relation with the ultimate good was not simply a matter of identifying the rightful object of human desire but actually demands an act (i.e., charity) that exceeds the powers of the natural activity of the human will to produce. The will has a passive potential for charity that God alone can actualize (actual grace) by operating immediately within the will (operative grace) to infuse the habit of charity (habitual grace) by which the human will cooperates with God (cooperative grace).[121] Cooperation with God is not caused by the knowledge of God given in revelation, the knowledge by which the natural desire for God has its proper object. It is caused by the Holy Spirit moving the will to love in a way that fulfills its nature but that is impossible apart from a right relation with God. Because there is no competitive relation between God and creatures, God's immediate movement of the will does not violate the will's freedom, which can embrace the means by which God's grace comes to flourish in the creature.

Lonergan's careful reading of Aquinas on operative grace (aided by Landgraf and Lottin) reveals the problem that remains at the heart of de Lubac's and Rahner's accounts of grace. Aquinas recognized that the intellect's mere specification of the proper object of the natural desire for God was insufficient to sustain the distinction between grace and creation. In fact, Lonergan underscores that Aquinas correctly identified this assumption as unwittingly Pelagian and sought to correct it for that reason. De Lubac's and Rahner's accounts simply return the issue to a position in which the will is a passive potency, sin is ignorance, and knowledge of the good is presumed to imply the ability to perform it.

Summarily, de Lubac's and Rahner's accounts of the unity of grace and creation suffer from three confusions. First, "supernatural" principally means, for them, the infinite excess of intellectual desire, which remains discontent with every finite, natural object. The appeal to the a priori grace bestowed on nature vitiates the original meaning of the concept, which supplied an important way to distinguish the gratuity of grace from creation. Indeed, overcoming the separation of grace from creation as it was maintained by neo-scholastic theology was their primary concern and motivation. Second, as a result of the unrecognized muddle this introduces into the concept of the supernatural, God's self-communication in creation is conflated with grace itself. Rahner makes this claim explicit, preferring that God's self-communication be equated with grace and that all grace be understood as uncreated. In de Lubac, even the theoretical differentiation that Rahner maintains with the hypothesis of a "pure" nature is rejected by de Lubac in preference for emphasizing the ontological reality of the summons to union with God, which is a gratuity that can be distinguished from the decision to create but is everywhere coincident with the actuality of created being. Finally, these two confusions are also bound up with an overly intellectualist conception of human freedom, which makes the intellect the ground of human freedom, renders the will a purely passive potency, and presumes that sin is derived from error and that knowledge of the good is sufficient for its performance.

The fundamental mistake that animates these three appears to be that possessing a singular, supernatural destiny entails an affirmation that creation is graced a priori. Apart from the right object for that desire, it will remain unrealized. But because humanity always anticipates its final end in every intellectual act, the mere specification of the right object of desire is sufficient for its attainment, based on the prior grace given in creation and the call. Neo-scholasticism argued that the gratuity of grace demanded both a natural and supernatural goal, which de Lubac and Rahner rightly rejected in favor of the singular, supernatural destiny of spiritual creatures revealed in the intellect. But what their lack of a coherent conception of the will made them unable to sustain was a way to affirm this supernatural dynamism of the human person together with the natural inability to produce the act necessary to attain that end, even with the knowledge of the right object.

Uniting Creation and Grace in a Metaphysical Ontology

These mistakes do not eliminate the possibility of maintaining the separation of creation from grace. One could easily find examples throughout de Lubac's and Rahner's writings in which the difference between grace and creation is upheld and strongly asserted. De Lubac's theology in particular, because he understands the offer of grace as a historical and not transcendental reality, can even more strongly claim to uphold the notion that we have a supernatural destiny that we are unable to fulfill by our own powers. According to de Lubac, historical revelation actually discloses the true object of our natural desire for the supernatural, and this object does not reside even potentially in human consciousness.[122] It must be received from God. But even this explanation equates having a supernatural goal, which necessarily exceeds every finite object, with the presence of grace within human nature. The yearning inscribed on the creature's being is already the work of grace, prior even to the arrival of its fulfillment.

My intent in this chapter is not to deny that de Lubac and Rahner make the distinction between grace and creation, but that their way of uniting them cannot be sustained because of grace beneath creation. Creation will accordingly, though unwittingly, dictate the meaning and content of grace. Grace will be incapable of exercising any critical relation to what is considered the "natural" created order, or of introducing any content not already presupposed within creation. The Thomist dictum "Grace perfects nature" is understood as the sanctioning and ratification of what is essentially given in creation.

This draws my analysis back to the discussion of intuition in the previous chapter. A union of creation and grace that is established in a preconceptual intuition will lack a critical concept by which to submit to transformation the interpretation of what is natural to the created order. In Aquinas, the way was opened to such a concept through the idea of the supernatural, which distinguished the gratuity of grace from the gratuity of creation. But in the absence of this critical concept, the distinction between grace and creation can be only abstractly and negatively sustained. In de Lubac, the twofold gratuity of creation and grace is a delineation that is made strictly as an abstraction within the affirmation of their singular, ontological identity in created being. As he famously said, reversing Maritain's maxim, "Unite in order to distinguish properly."[123] Rahner also maintains the theoretical union of grace with creation, except for him their union is known in transcendental experience. As with de Lubac, the revelation given in transcendental experience is distributed in the categorical revelation of history. But where de Lubac emphasizes the ontological identity of the two in creation and locates the differentiation in God, Rahner locates both the union and the differentiation in consciousness. The difference between the two is explained by de Lubac's reduction of subjectivity to ontology and Rahner's insistence on the necessity of preserving subjectivity.

If the trouble is that both accounts cannot sustain a coherent differentiation of grace from creation, then it appears dubious to suggest that this problem arises because these accounts have actually reinforced the separation they are attempting to overcome. But insofar as grace is assimilated to nature and subsumed beneath creation, it is not actually the union of creation and grace that is being thought. It is an abstract differentiation of aspects of a single reality in which what is "natural" is simply what is immediately given in the experience of the world. The content of grace is the experience of creation, and the two are differentiated only abstractly. This means that neither de Lubac's ontology nor Rahner's transcendental analysis attains a real union, even in intuition. Rather, they preserve the separation of grace from creation in a negative relation of abstract identity.

Another important point must be made on the priority of intuition. The assumption is not just that the abstract union preserves the separation, but also that the immediate union of grace with creation, which is understood to be concrete, is unconscious of the fragmented social relation on which it depends. The separation that is both abstractly established and preserved is also a repetition of a actually existing separation in historical existence. To claim that the two are united immediately in creation occludes recognition of this continued fragmentation in sociohistorical reality, which are the social relations determined by bourgeois property right. It remains naive—or, as Hegel said, "blind"—to its own reinforcing of the separation it believes it is overcoming. The true union of grace with creation, then, must take the form of an actual historical social alternative to this fragmentation.

The difficulty we have been tracing throughout this chapter is that the union of grace with creation in Western theology demands precise metaphysical distinctions between the supernatural and the natural and between the will and the intellect. An immediate union of grace with creation, in being or consciousness, will enshrine the opposition of the two doctrines rather than reconciling them. In doing so, the social relations that perpetuate that separation will also be reinforced, and the social and material significance of grace will be completely lost. The Protestant model of grace, specifically the doctrines of justification and election, should be understood as responses to this failure of the metaphysical categories of Catholic theology to adequately attend to the social dimension of grace. This Protestant model is the subject of the next chapter.

Notes

1. These essays of Henri de Lubac are, chronologically, "Apologetic et théologie," *Nouvelle Revue Théologique* 57 (1930): 361–78; "Deux Augustiniens fourvoyés: Baius et Jansenius," *Recherches des Science Religieuse* 21 (1931): 422–33, 513–40; and "Remarques sur l'histoire du mot 'Surnaturel,'" *Nouvelle Revue Théologique* 61 (1934): 350–70. It is significant that Lubac mentions the prior publication of the first three chapters on Baius and Jansenius only in his memoirs. See Henri de Lubac, *At the Service of the Church: Henri De Lubac Reflects on the Circumstances That Occasioned His Writings*, trans. Anne Elizabeth Englund (San Francisco: Communio, 1993), 35–36. See also Joseph A. Komonchak, "Theology and Culture at Mid-Century: The Example of Henri de Lubac," *Theological Studies* 51, no. 4 (1990): 579–81.

2. The conclusion occurs in Henri de Lubac, *Surnaturel: Études historiques* (Paris: Aubier, 1946), 483–94. See Bernard J. F. Lonergan, *Phenomenology and Logic: The Boston College Lectures on Mathematical Logic and Existentialism*, ed. Frederick E. Crowe and Philip McShane, Collected Works of Bernard Lonergan 18 (Toronto: University of Toronto Press, 2001), 350. I am indebted to Dr. Paul DeHart for calling this passage to my attention.

3. Reginald Garrigou-Lagrange, "La nouvelle théologie où va-t-elle?," *Angelicum* 23 (1946): 126–45.

4. I believe it is basically valid to suggest that, in the main, the teaching of Vatican II reflects acceptance of both transcendental Thomism's and the new theology's critiques of neo-scholasticism.

5. These theologians range from those who continue to use the term to refer to anything "out of the ordinary" to those who are referring to the unity of God and creation.

6. All but one of the relevant articles by Landgraf were collected, often with significant revisions, in Artur Michael Landgraf, *Dogmengeschichte der Frühscholastik*, vol. 1 (Regensburg, Ger.: Pustet, 1952). The following supplies the original journal citations for the articles, followed by the *Dogmengeschichte* page numbers in brackets: "Die Erkenntnis der heiligmachenden Gnade in der Frühscholastik," *Scholastik* 3 (1928): 28–64 [202–14]; "Studien zur Erkenntnis des Übernatürlichen in der Frühscholastik," *Scholastik* 4 (1929): 1–37, 189–220, 352–89 [141–201]; "Die Erkenntnis der helfenden Gnade in der Frühscholastik," *Zeitschrift für Katholische Theologie* 55 (1931): 177–238, 407–37, 562–91 [51–140]. See also Landgraf, "Grundlagen für ein Verständnis der Bußlehre der Früh- und Hochscholastik," *Zeitschrift für Katholische Theologie* 51 (1927): 161–94; and Bernard J.F. Lonergan, *Grace and Freedom: Operative Grace in the Thought of St Thomas Aquinas*, vol. 1, *Collected Works of Bernard Lonergan* (Toronto: University of Toronto, 2000), 1–20, 162–92. Additionally, the work of Odon Lottin is equally significant on the question of human liberty. See "Les définitions du libre arbitre au douzième siècle," *Revue Thomiste* 10 (1927): 104–20, 214–30; "La théorie du libre arbitre pendant le premier tiers du Xiiie siècle," *Revue Thomiste* 10 (1927): 350–82; "Le traité du libre arbitre depuis le Chancelier Phillipe jusqu'à saint Thomas D'aquin," *Revue Thomiste* 10 (1927), 446–72; and "Liberté humaine et motion divine," *Recherches de Théologie Ancienne et Médiévale* 7 (1935): 52–69, 156–73.

7. Lonergan, *Grace and Freedom*.

8. See Landgraf, *Dogmengeschichte Der Frühscholastik* and the discussion in Lonergan, *Grace and Freedom*, 1–20, 162–92.

9. Lonergan, *Grace and Freedom*, 44–45, quoted in J. Michael Stebbins, *The Divine Initiative: Grace, World-Order, and Human Freedom in the Early Writings of Bernard Lonergan* (Toronto: University of Toronto Press, 1995), 68.

10. Landgraf, "Studien zur Erkenntnis," 14–15 and n. 1 [150–51].

11. Lonergan, *Grace and Freedom*, 41. See also Stebbins, *Divine Initiative*, 69–74.

12. Lonergan, *Grace and Freedom*, 15.

13. Ibid., 181–91; and Stebbins, *Divine Initiative*, 67–78.

14. Landgraf, " Studien zur Erkenntnis," 374n3, 352–89 [194, 183–201].

15. Lonergan, *Grace and Freedom*, 17. See also Stebbins, *Divine Initiative*, 71–72.

16. See Landgraf, " Studien zur Erkenntnis," 381–82. See also Stebbins, *Divine Initiative*, 78.

17. Lonergan, *Grace and Freedom*, 14–20; Landgraf, " Studien zur Erkenntnis," 214, 374, 377, 381–84 [180, 194, 197, 197–99].

18. See Landgraf, " Studien zur Erkenntnis," 374 [194]; and Lonergan, *Grace and Freedom*, 184–90. On the Stoic origins of this idea, see Dieter Henrich, "The Basic Structure of Modern Philosophy," *Cultural Hermeneutics* 22 (1974): 1–18.

19. Landgraf, " Studien zur Erkenntnis," 381–82 [197–99]. See also Stebbins, *Divine Initiative*, 78–79.

20. Grace was specified according to its effects as healing (*sanans*), elevating (*elevans*), habitual, and actual. Both actual and habitual graces must have an operative aspect (in which God alone is working) and a cooperative aspect (in which God and the creature are working). See Thomas Aquinas, *Summa theologiae* 1-2.111. All citations to the *Summa theologiae* are taken from *The Summa Theologiae of St. Thomas Aquinas*, trans. Fathers of the English Dominican Province, 2nd ed. (Notre Dame, IN: Christian Classics, 1981); henceforth cited as *ST*.

21. Landgraf, "Studien zur Erkenntnis," 381–82 [197–99]. See also Stebbins, *Divine Initiative*, 78–79..

22. Stebbins, *Divine Initiative*, 79.

23. This idea points to the distinction between uncreated and created grace, which will be important in our discussion of Rahner in this chapter. That is, uncreated grace is participation in God's own life, whereas created grace effects transformation of the creature that makes possible this participation.

24. See Stebbins's full discussion of Lonergan's assessment of Philip the Chancellor's achievement in *Divine Initiative*, 73–83.

25. "Le désir qui jaillit de ce 'fond' de l'âme est un désir 'par privation' et non par 'commencement de possession.'" De Lubac is here citing Auguste-Joseph-Alphonse Gratry, *De la conaissance de Dieu*, 2nd ed. (n.p., 1854), 2:310–11. Henri de Lubac, *The Mystery of the Supernatural*, trans. Rosemary Sheed, Milestones in Catholic Theology (New York: Crossroad, 1998), 84. The French edition is *Le mystère du surnaturel*, Oeuvres Complètes (Paris: Cerf, 2000), 116. Subsequent citations include page numbers of the French edition in brackets.

26. Thomas Aquinas, *Summa contra Gentiles*, trans. Vernon J. Bourke (South Bend, IN: University of Notre Dame Press, 1956), 3.57.4.

27. Aquinas, *ST* 1.12.1. See also *De veritate* 8.3.12,20.11.7, 18.1.5.

28. The reader should consult Gerald A. McCool, *Catholic Theology in the Nineteenth Century: The Quest for a Unitary Method* (New York: Seabury, 1977), 1–36. His discussion of the background for nineteenth-century Roman Catholic theology, together with the combined influence of *Dei Filius* and *Aeterni Patris* for neo-scholasticism, is invaluable for properly understanding what de Lubac was rejecting and affirming in the theology of his day. This is especially significant with regard to his attitude to modernity, as will be shown presently. Stephen Duffy also makes significant points concerning de Lubac's critique of post-Tridentine Roman Catholic theology. See Stephen J. Duffy, *The Dynamics of Grace: Perspectives in Theological*

Anthropology (Collegeville, MN: Liturgical, 1993), 50–84. My reading of de Lubac is informed by both these texts.

29. De Lubac's project is largely an attemp to retrieve the sense of the sacred that modern culture had lost. Endeavors such as *Sources chrétiennes* and the volumes on medieval exegesis, ought to be seen as de Lubac's attempt to cultivate a renewed sense of the sacred. See Henri de Lubac, *Medieval Exegesis*, Ressourcement (Grand Rapids, MI: Eerdmans, 1998). The French is *Exégèse médiévale; Les quatre sens de l'écriture*, Théologie (Paris: Aubier, 1959).

30. Henri de Lubac, *Theology in History*, trans. Anne Englund Nash (San Francisco: Ignatius, 1996), 224–25. The French is *Théologie dans l'histoire*, vol. 2, *Questions disputées et résistance au Nazisme* (Paris: Brouwer, 1990).

31. Reflected in Henri de Lubac, *The Drama of Atheistic Humanism* (New York: Sheed & Ward, 1950). The French is *Le drame de l'humanisme athée*, Oeuvres Complètes (Paris: Cerf, 1998). Another translation is *The Drama of Atheist Humanism*, trans. Edith M. Riley, Anne Englund Nash, and Mark Sebanc (San Francisco: Ignatius, 1995). This should be linked to McCool's analysis of romantic French traditionalism in *Catholic Theology in the Nineteenth Century*, 37–58. Together, these elements help us to see why de Lubac's critics often accused him and his allies of "modernism," despite his shared distaste for modernity. In this respect, as I will argue, de Lubac's is a more "radical" conservative reaction inasmuch as it represents a rejection of modernity *tout court*. De Lubac significantly expands the traditionalist critique of rationalism to show how theologians themselves were at least partially responsible. On this point, see Joseph A. Komonchak, "The Enlightenment and the Construction of Roman Catholicism," *Annual of the Catholic Commission on Intellectual and Cultural Affairs* (1985): 31–59.

32. See also de Lubac, *Theology in History*, 224–34. There, de Lubac notes that ecclesiastical leadership is culpable for this as well. This is also, in part, the argument of *The Drama of Atheist Humanism*.

33. De Lubac, *Theology in History*, 230. De Lubac is in essential agreement with neo-scholasticism in claiming that rationalism is to blame for the alienation of religion and spirituality from modern culture. He makes this clear in "Internal Causes," in which he isolates four such causes, each of which is due to a fundamental theological failure. These are the contrast between secular knowledge and religious instruction, the fact that post-Reformation Roman Catholic theology was defined by its opposition to heresies and errors, the separation of nature from the supernatural, and the predominance of a rationalistic spirit in ecclesial and broader culture. Henri de Lubac, *Mémoire sur l'occasion de mes écrits*, ed. Georges Chantraine and Fabienne Clinquart, Oeuvres Complètes (Paris: Cerf, 2006), 188–89.

34. Aristotle, *Politics* 1253a8. The context is the discussion of nature.

35. Henri de Lubac, *The Mystery of the Supernatural*, 144–45.

36. See de Lubac, *At the Service of the Church*, 18–21, 35, 64–65. The French is *Mémoire sur l'occasion de mes écrits*. Also see Bruno Forte, "Nature and Grace in Henri de Lubac: From *Surnaturel* to *Le mystère du surnaturel*," *Communio* 23, no. 4 (1996): 725–37. Forte notes the significance of Antonio Russo, *Henri de Lubac: Teologia e dogma nella storia; L'influsso di Blondel* (Rome: Studium, 1990). See also Henri de Lubac, *Theological Fragments* (San Francisco: Ignatius, 1989), 377–404. The French is *Théologies d'occasion* (Paris: Brouwer, 1984). De Lubac was exposed to conversations surrounding the work of Blondel, Maréchal, and Rousselot as a student in the 1920s and 1930s. De Lubac learned from these three (especially Rousselot and Maréchal) to emphasize a theological a priori in human intellection and the dynamism of subjectivity. This anthropological emphasis is his framework for conceiving the coincidence of human nature and the supernatural as the *imago Dei*. But beyond this, Blondel's "method of immanence" was clearly important in helping de Lubac to seize upon the importance of concrete, historical human being in *Surnaturel*.

37. See Komonchak, "Theology and Culture at Mid-Century," 579–602.

38. de Lubac appears to have recognized this. Three years later, he published the independent essay "La mystère du surnaturel," which he said was "not a repetition or refinement, but a complement to the book." See Henri de Lubac, *The Splendour of the Church*, Denus Books (Glen Rock, NJ: Paulist, 1963), 62. The essay "The Mystery of the Supernatural" contains none of the paradoxical language of *Surnaturel* but makes its argument quite clearly. It is collected in de Lubac, *Theology in History*, 281–316.

39. "Avant donc d'aimer Dieu, et pour pouvoir l'aimer, il desire" (de Lubac, *Surnaturel*, 483). Subsequent references to this source will be cited in the text.

40. "Si ce désir exige, au sense que nous avons dit, d'être comblé, c'est que déjà Dieu meme est à sa source, bien qu'encore 'anonyme.' Désir naturel du surnaturel: c'est en nous l'action permanente du Dieu qui crée notre nature, comme la grace est en nous l'action permanente du Dieu qui crée l'ordre moral. Ordre de la 'nature' et ordre de la 'moralité,' ces deux orders condtiennent toutes les conditions—les unes essentielles et nécesires, les autres personnelles et libres,—propres à nous faire atteindre notre fin surnaturelle, et tous deux sont continues à l'intérieur d'un meme monde, d'un monde unique, qu'on peut appeler pour cela meme, quoiqu'il continenne des elements tout naturels, monde surnaturel" (ibid., 487).

41. De Lubac will refer positively to Maréchal's avowal of Aquinas' claim that God is known implicitly in every act of knowing, placing him in agreement with Rahner on this point. See de Lubac, *The Discovery of God*, 35. The French is *De la connaissance de Dieu*, 2nd ed. (Paris: Témoignage Chrétien, 1948). This is repeated in its expanded version, Henri de Lubac, Georges Chantraine, and Emmanuel Tourpe, *Sur les chemins de Dieu*, Oeuvres Complètes Henri De Lubac (Paris: Cerf, 2006), 44–45 and 273n1. This is what de Lubac means when he invokes the patristic tradition in order to link the natural desire for God directly to the fact that human beings are the image of God in salvation history. It is clear that de Lubac's thinking at this point remains tied to Maréchal's transcendental analysis of the dynamism of human intellection. He has simply made the very important move here of associating this desire directly with the idea of the image of God in patristic theology as a way of attempting to pry the notion loose from the restrictions placed on it by Aristotelian Thomism, linking it to an account of salvation history. On this point, see the discussion by Hans Urs von Balthasar, The Theology of Henri de Lubac: An Overview (San Francisco: Ignatius, 1991).

42. The controversy was particularly acute in that these claims were made explicit by Reginald Garrigou-Lagrange in his now famous essay "La nouvelle théologie où va-t-elle?

43. See Stephen J. Duffy, *The Graced Horizon: Nature and Grace in Modern Catholic Thought* (Collegeville, MN: Liturgical, 1992), 59–65. The reader should also consult the discussion of Rahner in Duffy, *Dynamics of Grace*.

44. Duffy, *Graced Horizon*, 62. See also Karl Rahner, "Concerning the Relationship between Nature and Grace," in *Theological Investigations*, ed. Cornelius Ernst (New York: Crossroad, 1983), 1:304. Henceforth, references to the different volumes of Rahner's *Theological Investigations* will be abbreviated as *TI*, followed by the volume and page number.

45. See Duffy, *Graced Horizon*, 59–65.

46. It is important here to note the distinction between the creature having all that is necessary to fulfill its goal and having all that is necessary to respond to God's grace. De Lubac makes it clear that the natural human being cannot fulfill its goal unaided, but he presumes that the natural will, animated by this desire, possesses the power to respond even to this offer. This assumption will prove to be problematic.

47. I have already noted the important essay "La mystère du surnatural," which appeared in 1949; but the most important is the publication of Henri de Lubac, *Augustinianism and Modern Theology*, trans. Lancelot Capel Sheppard (New York: Crossroad, 2000). The French is *Augustinisme et théologie moderne*, Théologie (Paris: Aubier, 1965).

48. John Milbank, *The Suspended Middle: Henri de Lubac and the Debate concerning the Supernatural* (Grand Rapids, MI: Eerdmans, 2005). Milbank significantly misinterprets both the events of de Lubac's biography and the nature of the argument of the conclusion of *Surnaturel*.

The irony of this lies with the fact that de Lubac's earlier argument is more closely tied to transcendental Thomism—a school of thinking for which Milbank has been anything but supportive in print.

49. Guy Mansini, "Henri de Lubac, the Natural Desire to See God, and Pure Nature," *Gregorianum* 83, no. 1 (2002):89–109. N.B., the three points to which I am directing the readers attention appear as a subpoint of five larger points Mansini makes regarding de Lubac's arguments. These specific subpoints occur on pp. 90–91, beneath his fourth point.

50. Guy Mansini, "Henri de Lubac, the Natural Desire to See God, and Pure Nature," 90–91.

51. Ibid., 91. This kind of claim is what would attract von Balthasar to de Lubac, against Rahner, whom he thought treated the desire as anthropologically recognizable.

52. Mansini, 91.

53. Mansini, 91.

54. For discussion of the impact of *Humani Generis* on de Lubac's argument, see ibid. See also the discussion in Duffy, *Dynamics of Grace*, 59–65.

55. See de Lubac, *Mystery of the Supernatural*, 54–56 [80–83]. This marks an attempt to move away from the transcendentalized analysis of the human person in the earlier work. The critique of Rahner becomes, as it were, an unstated critique of his own earlier position. As McCool notes in relationship to Rahner, the tendency to associate the dynamism of human being with the natural desire for God was a result of the combined influence of Maréchalian and Augustinian themes. This, indeed, appears to be the case with the early de Lubac, who subsequently altered those assumptions after his engagement with Rahner and the issuance of *Humani Generis*. See Gerald A. McCool, *The Theology of Karl Rahner* (Albany, NY: Magi, 1961), 14. Note also de Lubac's claims regarding the knowledge of the desire only in light of revelation in chapter 11 of *Mystery of the Supernatural* (207–21 [257–72]).

56. Mansini's summary in "Henri de Lubac" brings out the fact that the most important aspect of *Mystery of the Supernatural* is that its fundamental claims about the natural desire to see God are not significantly different from those in *Surnaturel*. What has changed is that, after *Humani Generis*, de Lubac no longer held that an intellectual creature could be understood to have only a supernatural end. Indeed, Mansini notes, along with J. F. X. Knasas, "The Liberationist Critique of Maritain's New Christendom," *Thomist* 52 (1988): 254n19, that the more nuanced position of *Mystery of the Supernatural* appears to be not that there could not have been an intellectual creature without a supernatural end but that it was possible to conceive of an intellectual creature without such an end only as a transcendentalized abstraction. De Lubac continued to maintain that the natural desire for the supernatural was itself unconditional and absolute, and he did so in a more forceful fashion than in *Surnaturel* by emphasizing the concrete history of salvation much more in his later work. See Mansini, "Henri de Lubac," 94n14.

57. This claim is the opposite of John Milbank's thesis in *Suspended Middle*.

58. See de Lubac, *Mystery of the Supernatural*, 62, 183 [90, 227–28].

59. Ibid., 82–82 [113–14]. See also de Lubac's argument for the rejection of essential and existential orders (64–67 [92–96]).

60. de Lubac, *Surnaturel*. This is the principal argument of chapter 6 of *Mystery of the Supernatural*, "The Christian Paradox of Man" (101–18).

61. Lubac, *Mystery of the Supernatural*, 76–77 [106–8]. de Lubac also refers to a "twofold call inscribed by God in the very make-up of these creatures" (*Mystery of the Supernatural*, 130 [68]).

62. De Lubac, *Mystery of the Supernatural*, 62, 72 [90, 103].

63. Ibid., 64–67 [92–96].

64. Ibid., 80–81 [112–13].

65. See ibid., 119–39 [55–77].

66. On this point, it is imperative that the reader recognize the distinction that de Lubac draws, in both his early and late work, between "nature" as the ontological principle of necessity within which God's call is expressed and "morality" as the domain of freedom within which the

offer of grace is received and accepted. As he says, ibid., 183 [227–28]: "Though one cannot reduce everything to the clarity of a simple vision free of all mystery, one can at least advance dialectically to the harmony which lies beyond the apparent opposition. And this will be easier if, taking the notion of God's transcendence with total seriousness, we stop seeing the call to the supernatural and the offer of grace in a chronological series, as though the second is governed by the first: as though God were bound by his own call once uttered, and could not then recall his offer. The offer of grace expresses, in the sphere of moral liberty, the same act of divine loving kindness that the call to the supernatural expresses in the ontological sphere. Thus there is nothing in the former to diminish beforehand in any way the gratuitousness of the latter. Neither is exterior to the other, and therefore neither comes before the other. There is always the same unique sovereign initiative at work in both, and the only difference lies in relation to us, because we are at once nature and liberty, and ontological tendency and a spiritual will." This passage should be compared with the quotations in the text. Note the same association of ontology with necessity, desire, and call, as well as morality with freedom, will, and response. De Lubac also links these two orders (without naming him) to Philip the Chancellor's distinction between natural and elicited appetites (*Mystery of the Supernatural*, 182 [226].) Note the tendency in both passages to insist that these are but two facets of the same experience of the one divine act. As De Lubac said earlier, the ontological and moral orders "contain every condition . . . proper to attending to our supernatural end, and both are contained at the interior of the same world, of a unique world, which we can even call . . . a supernatural world" (*Surnaturel*, 487.)

67. Rahner, "Concerning the Relationship," in *TI*, 1:296–317.

68. *Humani Generis* did not mention de Lubac by name, and Rahner's essay refers merely to "D," but it was clear that both the encyclical and the essay were referring to positions that were at least associated with de Lubac himself.

69. Karen Kilby, *Karl Rahner: Theology and Philosophy* (New York: Routledge, 2004), 70–99.

70. The point is made by Duffy, *Dynamics of Grace*, 262–75. Also see the discussion of Rahner in Duffy, *Graced Horizon*. As with de Lubac, my discussion of Rahner is marked by my reading of Duffy's excellent accounts. The same point is also made by Francis P. Fiorenza, "Karl Rahner and the Kantian Problematic," the introduction to Karl Rahner, *Spirit in the World*, trans. William Dych (New York: Continuum, 1994), xxvii–xlv.

71. Rahner, *Spirit in the World*, 92–97. German taken from Karl Rahner, "*Geist im Welt*," [German] in *Sämtliche werke*, vol. 2, ed. Karl-Rahner-Stiftung and Karl Lehmann (Freiburg im Breisgau, Ger.: Herder, 1995), 79–83.

72. Rahner, *Spirit in the World*, 78–82 [69–72]. The German page numbers are bracketed.

73. Rahner, *Spirit in the World*, 81.

74. Ibid., 81 [71].

75. For this point, see Carmichael C. Peters, *A Gadamerian Reading of Karl Rahner's Theology of Grace and Freedom* (Lanham, MD: Catholic Scholars Press, 2000), 285–91 and 99–306.

76. Rahner, *Spirit in the World*, 57–77 [54–68].

77. Ibid., 68–71 [62–64].

78. Ibid., 81, 406–8 [71, 298–300].

79. Ibid., 135–45, 54–56, 202–36 [111–18, 24–25, 57–80].

80. Ibid.

81. Ibid., 393–408 [290–300].

82. On this point, see Peters, *Gadamerian Reading*, 299–306.

83. See Rahner, *Spirit in the World*, 387–408 [286–300]. See also Karl Rahner, *Hearer of the Word: Laying the Foundation for a Philosophy of Religion*, trans. Andrew Tallon (New York: Continuum, 1994), 1–9 [9–29]; and "Concerning the Relationship," in *TI*, 1:309–11, 15–17. The German page numbers are bracketed.

84. Rahner, "Concerning the Relationship," in *TI*, 1:304. See Duffy, *Graced Horizon*, 89–91.

85. See Rahner, "Concerning the Relationship," in *TI*, 1:303–10. See Duffy, *Graced Horizon*, 89–91.

86. Rahner, "Concerning the Relationship," in *TI*, 313–15.

87. See Thomas Aquinas, *ST* 1-2.109. This is the thesis of Karl Rahner in "Zur scholastischen Begrifflichkeit der ungeschaffenen Gnade," *Zeitschrift für Katholische Theologie* 63 (1939): 137–56. The English is "Some Implications of the Scholastic Concept of Uncreated Grace," in *TI*, 5:297–346. Rahner does this by emphasizing the priority of the divine self-communication over any created transformation prior to the reception of the Holy Spirit. He thus makes this transformation the effect of the Holy Spirit's presence, and not the prerequisite for that presence.

88. Rahner, "Some Implications," in *TI*, 5:320–24.

89. See Stephen J. Duffy, "Experience of Grace," in *The Cambridge Companion to Karl Rahner*, ed. Declan Marmion and Mary E. Hines, Cambridge Companions to Religion (New York: Cambridge University Press, 2005), 48.

90. Rahner, "Some Implications," in *TI*, 5:303, 312–17.

91. Ibid., 5:19–26 and 51–52.

92. Ibid., "Some Implications," 319–46.

93. Karl Rahner, *Foundations of Christian Faith: An Introduction to the Idea of Christianity*, trans. William V. Dych (New York: Seabury, 1978), 121. See the discussion of Rahner's deployment of uncreated grace in Peters, *Gadamerian Reading*, 320–29. See also the entry "Grace," in *Sacramentum Mundi: An Encyclopedia of Theology*, ed. Karl Rahner et al. (New York: Herder & Herder, 1968), 415–21.

94. Rahner, "Concerning the Relationship," in *TI*, 1:304–10.

95. The fact that this is a minor claim in the conclusion of *Surnaturel* but becomes the centerpiece of *The Mystery of the Supernatural* is most important for my argument.

96. De Lubac, *Mystery of the Supernatural*, 119–39. Yet de Lubac never offers any explanation of the meaning of this moment or its mechanics. It is the incomprehensibility of this moment that Milbank has sought to exploit in his own attempt to demonstrate the paradoxical coincidence of grace and creation. See Milbank, *Suspended Middle*.

97. Rahner, *Foundations of Christian Faith*, 121. See also Peters, *Gadamerian Reading*, 320–29.

98. Rahner, *Spirit in the World*, 135–45, 54–56, 202–36 [111–18, 24–25, 57–80].

99. An important point must be underscored here, because this reference to ontology might appear to contradict my earlier claim that the natural desire for the vision of God is simply a factual aspect of concrete intellectual experience rather than the ontological determination of human being. It is ontologically constitutive of human being that the intellect be dynamically structured to move out of itself and return to itself. However, it is simply a fact of intellectual experience that this dynamism is not satisfied with the self-presence displayed in the moment of abstraction but reaches beyond to an apprehension of Absolute Being. It is not a necessary aspect of intellectual experience as such. This is what marks, for Rahner, the difference between an intellect with a purely natural end and one with a supernatural one. This point is drawn out deftly by Peters, Gadamerian Reading, 299–306.

100. De Lubac, *Surnaturel*, 483.

101. De Lubac, *Surnaturel*. See de Lubac, *Mystery of the Supernatural*, 182. The reader should note that de Lubac explicitly refers to the distinction between the order of nature, which is the realm of "necessary connections," and that of elicited appetite, which is that of freedom. He here shows familiarity with Philip the Chancellor's distinction but misses its significance. As I will show, the entire point of Aquinas's development of this idea requires the notion of God's operation to infuse a habit into the creature, and not simply the idea that the habit itself can be freely acquired. De Lubac's understanding of freedom, along with Rahner's, requires an ontological conception of freedom that attempts to obviate this moment of infusion.

102. Henri de Lubac, *Pic de la mirandole: Études et discussions* (Paris: Aubier Montaigne, 1974), 174–75.

103. De Lubac, *Surnaturel*, 483.

104. The following discussion of Rahner's account of freedom is thoroughly indebted to Peters, *Gadamerian Reading*, esp. 306–20. His account supplies a superb overview and synthesis of the various places where Rahner discusses the will and human freedom.

105. See Rahner, *Spirit in the World*, 280–83.

106. Karl Rahner, "The Sin of Adam," in *TI*, 1:258. See Peters, *Gadamerian Reading*, 312–18.

107. See Peters, *Gadamerian Reading*, 290–99.

108. Rahner, *Hearer of the Word*, 68. See also Peters, ibid., 301–2. That affirmation is inseparable from the dynamism of human existence, which expresses the basic receptivity to Absolute Being.

109. This way of describing the matter is adopted from Vernon J. Bourke, *Will in Western Thought: An Historico- Critical Survey* (New York: Sheed & Ward, 1964), 193.

110. Lonergan, *Phenomenology and Logic*, 350.

111. John Milbank, *Theology and Social Theory: Beyond Secular Reason* (Malden, MA: Blackwell, 1993), 207ff.

112. Odon Lottin, *La theorie du libre arbitre depuis S. Anselme jusqu'a S. Thomas d'Aquin* (Louvain: St. Maximin, 1929); *Psychologie et Morale aux XIIe et XIIIe siècles*. 6 volumes. (Gembloux: Duculot, 1943–54), 1:221–62, 345–46, 374–75, 382–87 and 3:590–91; and see "La preuve de la liberté humaine chez Thomas d'Aquin," *Recherches de théologie ancienne et médiévale* 23 (1956): 325. In addition to Lonergan, the same argument was made and defended by Otto Pesch, "Philosophie und Theologie der Freiheit bei Thomas Aquin in quaest. Disp. 6 *De malo*" (Münchener Theologische Zeitschrift 13 (1962): 1–25; George Klubertanz, "The Root of Freedom in St. Thomas's Later Works" *Gregorianum* 42 (1961): 701–24; and Klaus Riesenhuber, "The Bases and Meaning of Freedom in Thomas Aquinas," in *American Catholic Philosophical Association* 48 (1974): 99–111 and *Die Tranzendenz der Freiheit zum Gutten: Der Wille in der Anthropologie und Metaphysik des Thomas von Aquin* (Munich: Berchmanskolleg Verlag, 1971). See the excellent summary of Lottin's position, with his own important elaboration on its consequences, in James F. Keenan, S.J., *Goodness and Rightness in Thomas Aquinas' Summa Theologiae* (Washington DC: Georgetown University Press, 1992), especially 21–61; and also Mary Jo Lozzio, *Self-Determination and the Moral Act: A Study of the Contribution of Odon Lottin, O.S.B.* (Louvain, Belg.: Peeters, 1995), 11–51. Both Keenan and Lozzio make important application of Lottin's ideas to contemporary moral theology.

113. Lonergan, *Grace and Freedom*, 92.

114. Ibid., 94–95. See also Stebbins, *Divine Initiative*, 84–92.

115. This is the exceptional insight of of James F. Keenan, S.J. in *Goodness and Rightness in Thomas Aquinas's Summa Theologiae* (Washington DC: Georgetown University Press, 1992).

116. For the issues discussed in this paragraph and the following, the reader should see the succinct discussion of the issues in James F. Keenan, *Goodness and Rightness in Thomas Aquinas's Summa theologiae* (Washington, DC: Georgetown University Press, 1992), 23–34.

117. Ibid., 38–56; Lonergan, 94–98; and Lozzio, *Self-Determination and the Moral Act*, 11–51.

118. See Lozzio, *Self-Determination and the Moral Act*, 28–35.

119. See the argument of Keenan, *Goodness and Rightness in Thomas Aquinas's Summa theologiae*.

120. See Lonergan, *Grace and Freedom*, 193–99.

121. Aquinas, *ST* 1-2.111.2.

122. This is what allows a thinker like Karen Kilbey to insist that de Lubac and Rahner are ultimately saying the same thing. See her argument in Karl Rahner, 116–19.

123. Jacques Maritain, *Distinguish in Order to Unite; or, The Degrees of Knowledge*, trans. Gerald B. Phelan (New York: Scribner, 1959).

3

Sin and Election

Protestant Theologies of Creation and Grace

Ernst Troeltsch reminded his readers in *Protestantism and Progress* that what we call Protestantism is an abstraction that developed as a shorthand description for disparate cultural, political, and theological concerns that appeared during the sixteenth-century fragmentation of European society.[1] Thinking of "Protestantism" as a distinct theological or ecclesial identity is a mistake, but one that appropriately, and ironically, captures its critical transgression of all fixed identities. As Paul Tillich argued, when the meaning of Protestantism shifted from "a political into a religious concept," the "Protestant element in Protestantism" became a "Protestant principle"

> that stands beyond all its realizations. It is the critical and dynamic source of all Protestant realizations, but it is not identical with any of them. . . . On the other hand, it can appear in all of them; it is a living, moving, restless power in them; and this is what it is supposed to be in a special way in historical Protestantism. The Protestant principle . . . contains the divine and human protests against any absolute claim made for a relative reality . . . [and] is the judge of every religious and cultural reality, including the religion and culture which calls itself "Protestant."[2]

The principle that this "Protestantism" demands is the rigorous imposition of the obligation to submit every regnant political, philosophical, theological, and ecclesial structure to scrutiny and to demand it justify its claim to authority. The heart of that demand is the disruptive event of God's grace, focused on God's justification of sinners and eternal decree of election.

For the Reformers, God's grace was radical and revolutionary. All authorities were subject to the absolute sovereignty of God's initiative over reality, but especially human justification. Ascribing absolute devotion to any relative reality was idolatry and must be exposed as such. The attempt to know God or to be saved apart from faith in God's initiative alone was just another manifestation of our broken, idolatrous relation to God. The highest manifestation of that broken relation was, for the Reformers, a church that perversely understood salvation as the usurpation of God's rightful prerogative for grace.

In response, the Reformers placed decisive emphasis on faith as the expression of a right relation to God, the fruit of justification. This socially conceived relation to God, which could be disordered by sin or redeemed by grace, preceded and determined all human knowledge and acts. The result was an altogether different framework for the theology of grace than the *caritas* soteriology of scholasticism. As Gerhard Ebeling remarked, Luther's theology of grace was not "based upon . . . [a] fundamental continuity between nature and grace":

> Certainly, Luther's view is not adequately represented by the mere negation of the hierarchical Thomist relationship between nature and grace. The difference which is unquestionably present clearly does not lie only in a different definition of the relationship between nature and grace, for it cannot be understood within the same conceptual scheme. The difficulty lies in the fact that the difference goes very much deeper than this. It is the basic concepts, or more precisely the fundamental questions they pose, which are different.[3]

Metaphysical concepts conform to a different paradigm than that of faith, which submits first to the authority of the word of God revealed in Scripture and proclamation.[4] Philosophy helped to interpret biblical concepts (such as sin, election, gospel, and law) and to show patterns of relation between them (for example, law/gospel and spirit/letter), but it could deceive where it served as a foundation for doctrine.[5]

Specifically, the Reformers rejected the idea that joining charity (*caritas*) to Aristotelian habit (*habitus*) was an accurate interpretation of Paul's theology of grace.[6] Luther insisted that the biblical doctrine of justification required a distinction between "person" and "work" that was impossible for Aristotelian ethics. In doing so, Luther lifted out the social reality of personhood, which precedes and conditions the character of personal acts. A person can be determined by sin and by grace—and before the final judgment she will be determined by both. Aristotle understood the formation of character in a way that lacked the critical account of the social determination of selfhood that Luther was developing, which chafed at the limitations imposed by the metaphysical concepts of potency and act. As Ebeling noted, Luther considered humanity first as *coram Deo*, according to that "passivity that constitutes man's being, as his existence as a creature, as his relations to God and his standing in the sight of God."[7] In these terms, grace was not the perfection of human potentiality but the restoration of humanity's broken relationship with God.[8] Luther insisted that this new relation is so significant that it amounts to a "substantial" transformation of humanity, as opposed to the merely "accidental" transformation envisioned by scholasticism. The creature's "substance" is determined by its relations to God and others.[9] The priority of social relation in Luther meant that sin deforms human nature and grace transforms it. Consequently, justification must be understood, first and last, as God's act to transform the relations of sin that condition all acts.

This emphasis on social relations in the Reformation theology of grace is far too often overlooked. As with Luther's doctrine of *theosis*, the oversight is largely due to Albrecht Ritschl's use of the neo-Kantian concept of "value" to interpret the Reformation doctrine of justification.[10] It is true that Protestant theologies of grace emphasized the individual (*pro me*) significance of grace, but this served specifically social and critical ends. Emphasis on the individual highlighted her irreducibility to metaphysical objectivity. This irreducibility opened up the critical standpoint with regard to metaphysics while bringing the intersubjectivity of the theology of grace into the foreground. Though medieval theology did not deny the social reality of grace, it could neither critically differentiate grace from the existing social relations that mediated it nor understand grace itself as a relational reality.

Luther lifts out both the social and critical dimension of grace in the *Disputation against Scholastic Theology* (1517). In that work, he used scholastics' categories to rupture their premises:

5. It is false to state that man's inclination is free to choose between either of two opposites. Indeed the inclination is not free, but captive. This is said in opposition to common opinion.

6. It is false to state that the will can by nature conform to correct precept. This is said in opposition to Scotus and Gabriel.

7. As a matter of fact, without the grace of God the will produces an act that is perverse and evil.

8. It does not, however, follow that the will is by nature evil, that is, essentially evil, as the Manicheans maintain.

9. It is nevertheless innately and inevitably evil and corrupt.

10. One must concede that the will is not free to strive toward whatever is declared good. This in opposition to Scotus and Gabriel.

11. Nor is it able to will or not to will whatever is prescribed. . . .

20. An act of friendship [with God] is done, not according to nature, but according to prevenient grace. This in opposition to Gabriel. . . .

29. The best and infallible preparation for grace and the sole disposition toward grace is the eternal election and predestination of God.

30. On the part of man, however, nothing precedes grace except indisposition and even rebellion against grace.[11]

What scholastic theology understands as the will's natural capacity to choose freely between good and evil, says Luther, is actually its determination by sin.[12] Because it is a social relation, the presence or absence of friendship with God determines human nature and does not derive from it. This does not mean that the will is naturally sinful, only that it is "innately and inevitably evil and corrupt," because it is conditioned by sin.[13] Apart from this friendship, the will is an "indisposition and even rebellion against grace." The friendship is established only by God's "eternal election and predestination." The will is meant for loving self-bestowal with God through grace, but it has been debased to mere self-preservation. Virtue ethics misidentifies this sinful condition of self-preservation with the goal of human nature:

38. There is no moral virtue without pride or sorrow, that is, without sin.

39. We are not masters of our actions, from beginning to end, but servants. This in opposition to the philosophers.

40. We do not become righteous by doing righteous deeds but, having been made righteous, we do righteous deeds. This in opposition to the philosophers.

41. Virtually the entire *Ethics* of Aristotle is the worst enemy of grace. This in opposition to the Scholastics. . . .

46. In vain does one fashion a logic of faith, a substitution brought about without regard for limit and measure. This in opposition to the new dialecticians. . . .

54. For an act to be meritorious, either the presence of grace is sufficient or its presence means nothing. This in opposition to Gabriel.[14]

Luther gives priority to the will's passivity, which leads him to oppose any sense that a sinful will acquires goodness by practical action. Rather, the will's acts (work) express the good or evil relation (person) to God and others that determine it.[15] Grace is the presence of this positive relation with God. Apart from that relation, the will only naturally acts sinfully. As Luther states, "The presence of grace is sufficient or its presence means nothing."[16]

Granting precedence to the relation reveals God's scandalous and paradoxical reversal of what is taken to be "natural," which is the source of the critical dimension. Attempting to ascend to knowledge of God through nature's glories (*theologia gloriae*), for Luther, unwittingly manifests a sinful relation to God, a disposition to "robbery."[17] But to receive in faith the promise given by God's self-communication in the cross (*theologia crucis*) is to experience the presence of grace, knowing God as God wills to be known.[18] The revelation of God in the cross confounds the "natural" drive to self-preservation and, in doing so, shows it to be an illusory foothold of sin.

If all good human acts express their right prior relation to God, then the central fact for Protestant theologies of grace is the divine election. As Michael Root has argued, all Protestant theologies of grace ask, "What must divine election be like if [its] assertions are true about the incapacity of the self for salvation and the total confidence the Christian may place in God?"[19] Though the doctrine was always vital to Protestant theology, it was Schleiermacher and Barth who made election central to resolving the separation of subject and object in modern theology. God's eternal decree of election, rather than the categories of nature and the supernatural, is the paradigm within which

Protestant theologies conceive the union of creation and grace. I will analyze the unities of grace and creation in Schleiermacher and Barth now in turn.

FRIEDRICH SCHLEIERMACHER

The world is the totality of antitheses; the
deity is the real negation of all antitheses.
—FRIEDRICH SCHLEIERMACHER

The orthodox Protestant formulations of the divine decree differ not in the priority they grant to election but in what they understand to be the ground (*fundamentum*) of election and its order of execution (*ordo salutis*).[20] Lutherans, Reformed Christians, and Jacob Arminius agree with one another that, as prior to all acts and merits, the decree of election precedes even creation.[21] They disagree with one another on whether the basis of election (*fundamentum electionis*) is in God's foreknowledge of the future faith of believers (*praevisa fides*), as the Lutherans and Remonstrants argued, or in the absolute decree (*decretum absolutum*) of the "deep recesses of the divine counsel" (*profunda illa divini consilii adyta*),[22] as the Reformed maintained.[23] On the basis of these different understandings of the ground of election, they also develop different understandings of predestination. Because they understand the ground of election to be God's foreknowledge of future faith, Lutherans and Arminius agree that God's eternal decree is universally to election, whereas it includes reprobation only in its execution.[24] But because the Reformed ground the decree in God's eternal divine counsel, God predestines to both election and reprobation. Lutherans and Remonstrants retained the medieval ordering of predestination, in which it was a special instance of God's general providence. The Reformed followed Calvin and made providence the execution of predestination.[25] In all three cases, however, the precedence of the decree over creation means that God's grace cannot be subsumed beneath creation. It is, instead, the execution of an eternal divine judgment in creation.

Additionally, all three schools in different ways recognize Jesus Christ as the "mirror of election" (*speculum electionis*). Jesus is the one in whom humanity sees and knows God's election.[26] As Barth comments, all doctrines of election know Christ as "the prototype and essence of . . . all divine electing and human election."[27] Christ is the basis for all sure knowledge that in faith God's grace is actual for me (*pro me*): "Whoever is elected is elected in Christ and only in Christ."[28]

Though election was always mediated solely by Jesus Christ, the order of its execution (*ordo salutis*) carried important theological implications, as I have already noted with the ground of election and predestination. Clarity on that order was important, because all traditional treatments of doctrinal loci were reconfigured to reflect the centrality of justification and the focus on election it demanded. A different logical order for the *ad extra* execution of God's eternal decree *ad intra* carried important dogmatic consequences.[29] But in each case, as Heinrich Heppe noted, the doctrine was focused on salvation in "the concrete existence and life of the world and of individual men with their complex of causes and effects."[30] Rather than fitting reality into general metaphysical categories, this search for precision in the doctrine of election was to understand the truth of existence solely through God's self-revelation in Christ. And, contrary to the common interpretation of Schleiermacher's theological project, this was exactly the approach taken by Schleiermacher, who cleared the path for the modern reconstruction of the doctrine as the unity of creation and grace.[31]

Like Rahner's, Schleiermacher's theology is inseparable from his general philosophical commitments. Making those commitments explicit, however, did not mean they were foundational.[32] As Manfred Frank has shown, "[S]trictly speaking, Schleiermacher does not have a metaphysics, if by this is meant a foundational philosophical doctrine."[33] Schleiermacher rejects the idea that "metaphysics could grasp the highest object of the human mind, or that it could exhaustively deal with the essential matter of the human spirit."[34] Philosophy reflects critically on consciousness only in order to identify the rules, as with Wittgenstein's "grammar" for thinking well and understanding how the mind acquires knowledge and recognizes its limits (1–11).[35] John Thiel's argument is that *The Christian Faith* is best understood as the application of these general rules for thought within the task of dogmatic theology. My concern is to bring into relief the relationship between these rules and the role of the doctrine of election in *The Christian Faith*.[36]

Schleiermacher divides consciousness in the *Dialectic* between an "organic function," concerned with objective sense impressions (reality), and an "intellectual function," corresponding with the spontaneous activity of subjectivity (ideality) (19–26).[37] The mind is the unity of these two functions, but these functions are dialectically contrasted to one another in the activity of thinking. The mind is aware of its immediate union with the world and itself, but neither of these can be represented accurately in thought (19–26, 51–52).[38] It is in the gap between the self and the world that thought happens, and the ideality of thought cannot overcome its separation from the real. The union of subject and object that precedes and determines thought, however, can be "felt." Schleiermacher analyzes this feeling in close detail in *The Christian Faith* as the "feeling of absolute dependence" (*das schlechthinnige Abhängigkeitsgefühl*), which all human beings share.[39]

Though thought cannot mediate the union of subject and object, it can construct a concept of that unity that precedes it. "World" is the mind's concept of its objectivity, the point at which thought can be described as pure sensation (43). The thought of the world is understood to include all that encompasses, conditions, and determines consciousness (24–25, esp. n. 34). It is the concept of "a totality made up of a plurality of specially relativized unities" (64) in which "the world and all that is in it stands under the form of contrast" (43). As Schleiermacher puts it in his 1822 lectures on the *Dialectic*, "[W]orld = unity with the inclusion of all contrasts."[40]

"God" is the concept at the opposite dialectical pole of "world." Whereas the world is the conceptual limit of thought determined by the organic function, "God" is the conceptual limit of the spontaneous self-determination of the intellectual function. "God" is the concept of absolute self-determination, unaffected by any objectivity. It is the philosophical concept of the "sphere of identity between" all contrasts, the "ideal germ of thinking" that "lacks the form of contrast" (64, 65). Or as Gerhard Speigler put it, God is the *non aliud* that is *totaliter aliter*[41]—that is, the Source of both the world and thought.[42] Schleiermacher succinctly stated in the 1822 lectures, "God = unity with the exclusion of all contrasts."[43]

"God" and "world" are codeterminants of all thought, but they represent different aspects of the single identity of subject and object that is the ground of all thought (39–41). "World" is the thought of that ground as an aggregate of contingent particulars, and "God" is the thought of that ground as absolute, without any contrast. The two concepts are mutually inclusive. The thought of God includes the world, and the thought of the world always includes God (33–41).

As I noted earlier, the awareness of the union of subject and nature is not in thought but in "feeling" (*Gefühl*).[44] This feeling is of immediate relative dependence on the world. It is a relative dependence because it includes an awareness of free self-determination as well.[45] But in the same way that the concept of the world includes the concept of God, the feeling of relative dependence includes a feeling of absolute dependence. The awareness of freedom is always conditioned by dependence, but the feeling of dependence is ultimately without contrast.[46] The world is the source of relative dependence, and God is the source (the "whence") of the feeling of absolute dependence.[47] God ruptures the presumption that self-identity derives from spontaneous self-determination.[48]

Philosophy has a general awareness of the concept of God as absolute, but it has no conceptual knowledge of God. It can merely deduce concepts from this awareness. As Jacqueline Mariña has noted, despite the fact that the self is immediately aware of its own unity, it only knows itself in its social relations.[49] True knowledge of God comes from the awareness of God through the practices, language, and culture of the church. The church gives conceptual content to preconceptual feeling. This content is the awareness of absolute dependence communicated by Jesus Christ, the Redeemer, and nurtured by the church.[50]

This cultural-linguistic dimension of Schleiermacher's understanding of doctrine is reflected in the relationship between the two parts of *The Christian Faith*.[51] The first part treats the most general form of pious Christian self-consciousness, which is the basic awareness of absolute dependence available even to philosophy. This awareness is superiorly cultivated and nurtured by the monotheistic religions. They mediate awareness of this universal dependence according to the doctrine of God's creation/preservation and providence and the knowledge of the divine attributes they give.[52]

The second part refracts this general awareness, expressed in creation and providence, through the special concepts of sin and grace (§§62–64). Schleiermacher declares that this special determination of absolute dependence "rest[s] upon a communication from the Redeemer, which we call Grace" (§63). Reception of this grace is also the believer's justification, because it describes "the situation of the individual in his transition from the corporate life of sinfulness to a living fellowship with Christ" (§107). Fellowship with Christ is transition from a sinful relation of antagonism to graceful fellowship with God (§63). Sin is an awareness of dependence determined by the corporate life of "the world," which seeks happiness only according to the relative contrasts of dependence and freedom (§§63, 65–74, 81). Redemption is that awareness determined by the fellowship with God communicated by Jesus Christ in the church (§63). As Schleiermacher states, the self only "look[s] at itself reflected in thought and find[s] a consciousness of God included there" in the "common life" of the Holy Spirit communicated in the church (§116.3, §§22–23).

In transitioning from sin to redemption, the Christian also becomes aware that the absolute dependence of all humanity (creation) is oriented to this fellowship with God (grace). This orientation of all creation to this goal of perfect fellowship with God is Schleiermacher's doctrine of election (§§115–25).[53] Knowledge of election is acquired within the contrast of sin and grace, where the totality of existence is understood to be a single, self-communicating decree of God in Christ.[54] The whole of world history is recognized by the Christian community as the execution of that decree (§§116, 64–69).[55] The whole of humanity is both elect and reprobate in that decree. Even human alienation is an integral element in the universal order that discloses this divine decree in Christ (§§116–17, 20, 64).[56]

Schleiermacher's doctrine of election synthesizes the Lutheran and Reformed perspectives.[57] He takes from Lutheranism the idea of a single decree but combines it with the Reformed idea of a double predestination. Instead of talking about elect and reprobate individuals, Schleiermacher ingeniously states that humanity in general is both reprobate and elect. In the same way that consciousness shuttles between subject and object, humanity is always simultaneously the justified and the sinners (*simul justus et peccator*) in Christ. It is only in Christ that awareness of absolute dependence is determined as God's eternal summons to fellowship.

Creation and grace are here different descriptions of the experience of existence.[58] But these experiences are united in the doctrine of election, which teaches that the general and special descriptions are united to give an account of the whole of reality as God's eternal self-communicating summons to fellowship with God through Jesus in the Christian community.[59]

Karl Barth

Karl Barth's relationship to Schleiermacher is notoriously complex. Though Barth railed against the liberal trajectory inaugurated by Schleiermacher's theology, he defended Schleiermacher from his most uncompromising detractors, such as Emil Brunner.[60] Many have recognized that Barth's agonistic struggle with Schleiermacher pit the two too easily against one another and blinded Barth's admirers to his debts to Schleiermacher.[61] Matthias Göckel has recently documented extensively the debt Barth owed to Schleiermacher's doctrine of election. Despite Barth's major innovations in the doctrine, his thought remains largely consistent with the ground cleared by Schleiermacher's single decree to election and reprobation in Christ.

Barth develops his doctrine of election in part 2 of *The Doctrine of God*, the second volume of *Church Dogmatics*.[62] In a long excursus passage in section 32 on the orthodox Protestant doctrine of election, Barth discusses the differences between the Lutheran, Reformed, and Remonstrant accounts. His own doctrine is a creative synthesis of what he believes are the most important aspects of each. He insists that Jesus Christ alone should be the basis for the doctrine, the electing God and elected human.

Barth approves of the Lutheran critique of the Reformed reference to God's "secret counsel," which declares, "The eternal predestination of God is to be considered in Christ, and in no way separately from Christ the mediator" (62). But Barth also defends Calvin and the Reformed against that critique, noting especially Calvin's claim that Christ is the "mirror of election." This idea, Barth says, "emphasises in the most drastic fashion the singularity of the election, and of the freedom in which God as Elector stands over against the elect" (63). Both schools, according to Barth, fail to draw the necessary conclusion of their focus on Christ alone. They maintain a residual abstractness in the doctrine. God's decision for salvation remains "independent of Jesus Christ and is only executed by Him." Jesus Christ is "a later and subordinate decision, while the first and true decision of election is to be sought . . . in the mystery of the self-existent being of God, and of a decree made in the absolute freedom of this divine being" (65). He is only the "organ which serves the electing will of God, as a means toward the attainment of the end foreordained for the elect" (67). Barth declares that Jesus Christ alone is both the first and last point of reference for election. He is the God who elects and the singular human being who is elected.

This focus on Jesus Christ lies at the heart of Barth's theology. It is what makes Jesus Christ the focal point for all true knowledge of God, humanity, and the world. In the decree of election, God predestines Godself to be God for humanity in Jesus Christ and predestines humanity to be God's covenant partner in Jesus Christ. In this way, Barth maintains the same codetermination of God and humanity as Schleiermacher. He agrees that "we can only speak about God by speaking about man." But he insists that this is not a general structure of human consciousness or a limit-concept of thought. "Rightly interpreted," Barth says, "it may be an expression of the true insight that God is not without man."[63] By this Barth means God's eternal election to be God as Jesus, and Jesus Christ himself as the elected human. His existence is the revelation of the truth of actuality. The whole of existence is the communication of his election.

God's decree of election precedes creation. Unlike Schleiermacher, Barth does not think of creation as a "general concept of a first cause or the final contingency of all things." In part 1 of *The Doctrine of Creation,* the third volume of *Church Dogmatics,* he continues: "[A] general conception of a common, supreme and final 'Whence of all things' will 'not suffice' as a statement of the Christian confession of 'an absolutely definite God'—who is also recognized as the Lord and Ruler of that history—and of that world's dependence on that God."[64] As a dogmatic claim, it is entirely distinguished from scientific and philosophical knowledge (3–41, esp. 22ff.). Because faith receives Jesus Christ as the self-communication of God's eternal Word, the doctrine of creation is associated for Barth with the proclamation of his lordship (22–34). Recognizing the world as God's creation is the result of first knowing it as the setting for the execution of God's eternal election of Jesus (29–31). We know God surely only in Jesus, and because of that knowledge we also know ourselves to be God's creatures (27–29).

Making election the basis for creation also informs Barth's exegesis of Genesis 1–3 (94–228). The Genesis accounts tell the "saga" (81–92) of humanity's encounter with God in the history of the covenant, and creation as its first work (60–81). The world is the "presupposition of the realization of the divine purpose of love in relation to the creature" (96), and "even the very existence and nature of the creature are the work of the grace of God" (95). The world is the "freely willed and executed positing of a reality distinct from God," which is specifically a "work of His love" in which God "wills . . . to reveal and manifest it [love] in His own co-existence with it [creation]" (95).[65]

This love is the "internal basis of creation" (228–329). Barth reads the second creation story as recounting the "history of creation from the inside" (232). It discloses that the creature "does not merely exist, but exists meaningfully," with a "purpose and plan and order" (229). Its purpose is "solely . . . [to be] the revelation of the glory of God's free love," of which creation is the "deed and event" (230). The creature is "intrinsically determined as the exponent of His glory . . . to become God's partner in this history" (230). That partnership is the creature's "benefit," "actualization," and "justification." It is benefit because creation's existence expresses God's benevolence (331ff); it is actuality because creation has its own reality distinct from God (341ff.); and the affirmation of the objective goodness of the creature's distinct existence is its justification (366ff.).

Election is fulfilled in reconciliation.[66] As Barth articulates its different aspects in *The Doctrine of Reconciliation,* the fourth volume of *Church Dogmatics,* the significance for humanity of Jesus's status as fully God and human, electing agent and elected object, is that he is "the Judge judged in our place" (reprobate), he is the "Royal Man" (elect) who brings true human fulfillment by liberating its freedom to affirm the covenant. All of humanity is elected in this one human being, because creation exists for the fellowship with God that he realizes. In this way, creation and grace are united solely in God's eternal election of Jesus Christ.

A Revealed Union: Concept, Sin, and Grace

As I noted in chapter 1, despite its emphasis on the extrinsic nature of grace, modern Protestant theology does not attempt, like Catholic neo-scholasticism, to evade transcendental subjectivity. Both Schleiermacher and Barth take Kant's critique of metaphysics for granted and interpret the legacy of Protestant theology in its light. Their interpretation of grace in terms of practical, critical reason shows this debt to Kant. It results in an extrinsic concept of grace that does not set objectivity in opposition to transcendental subjectivity but presupposes their separation and understands grace as the critical concept that, when imposed on the experience of this separation, unifies them. This unity is not an immediate intuition of metaphysical identity but a critical concept of the social relation that rightly mediates the opposition. The "natural" experience of subjectivity is of a social relation that mediates only its estrangement from reality. Grace is the critical concept imposed on that experience, received from the self-communication of God in Jesus Christ, which exposes the illusion of that social relation. Election is the doctrine that articulates the truth of existence as it is known from faith, which adopts the critical standpoint of grace as the normative criterion for interpreting the subjective experience of separation from nature. In faith, which stands within the imposition of grace on the experience of separation, the subject knows that this grace, which critically reveals the sinful illusion of our estrangement from reality, is identical with the truth that the world is God's creation. They are identical because they are different expressions of God's single decree of election.

Schleiermacher and Barth share this concern to recast the classical Protestant doctrine of election into a single decree of election and reprobation, which is relevant to the modern concern with the separation of the subject and nature. The important decisive difference between them concerns whether that critical role is fulfilled by the Christian community or by Jesus Christ. Schleiermacher focused on the subject's social relation to reality. All self-awareness is socially mediated, and an awareness shaped only by the immanence of "the world's" relative contrasts will lead inevitably to the alienation the church calls "sin." By contrast, the church's language, culture, and practices of grace shape a selfhood with faith in the absolute contrast-without-contrast, an awareness of the fellowship with God that determines all experience prior to the separation from nature.[67] In that faith, the natural experience of separation is known generally as creation/preservation and specifically as grace/sin, both of which are united in their identity with the doctrine of election. Grace is extrinsic because it is socially and not naturally apprehended, but it is subjective because it discloses the truth of the self's relation to nature.

Though he retains much of the form of Schleiermacher's reconstruction of election, Barth believes his doctrine is too abstract. Just as all prior doctrines of election failed to recognize the implications of claiming that Jesus was the sole mediator of election, Schleiermacher also misconceives election in general rather than special terms. As a result, he associates grace too closely with ecclesial mediation, leaving it insufficiently critical. Schleiermacher breaks with the Catholic conflation of social reality with metaphysical nature, but the church's culture, language, and practices are distinguished enough from this grace. Instead, election should be focused solely on the individual, Jesus of Nazareth. We must identify Jesus alone, not humanity in general, as the aim of God's decree. And in doing so, we must understand Jesus also as the agent of that decree, not some unknown "whence" of our absolute dependence. In Jesus alone, we know God to be never God apart from humanity, and in this we know that all of humanity is called by its existence as God's creature into the freedom of partnership with God that is possible in Christ. Associating this grace with the specific individual, Jesus, makes grace not only extrinsic but also objective. However, what is objectively true is the possibility for an intersubjective relation with Jesus Christ, which mediates the intersubjective reality of the covenant between God and humanity.

Both Schleiermacher and Barth retain the critical and social concept of grace that differentiates Protestant theology from metaphysics. That relational emphasis disrupts every subsuming of grace to creation. Even Schleiermacher, for whom intuition is pivotal, understands the practical life of the Christian community as the cultural-linguistic determination of that immediacy, which gives the conceptual form for its apprehension. Barth does not want to deny the general reality, but he refuses to allow it to control the field of theological affirmations. General humanity should not be the focus of election, except insofar as this is definitively known in relation to the specific person of Jesus Christ. Such a claim requires affirming that Jesus Christ alone determines the whole of existence, which is a more radical application of the antimetaphysical implications of the Protestant critique, and in a way that achieves a reduction of subjectivity to ontology that is similar to de Lubac's. Both theologians understand the truth of existence, disclosed in the critical standpoint of grace, to be the inherently social dimension of reality that emerges from the affirmation of the integral role of subjectivity in being.

It is this social dimension that leads Schleiermacher and Barth to place such high emphasis on spontaneous self-determination. Keeping with Protestant theology's indictment of self-preservation, both theologians identify this capacity for self-determination as the site of both alienation and liberation. Freedom of the will means the capacity for self-determination, and that capacity originates in subjective spontaneity.[68] In contrast to the emphasis on the Platonic immediacy of desire and the will in de Lubac and Rahner, Schleiermacher and Barth focus on the constructive, practical activity of the self, which is more Cartesian.[69] Freedom resides not in the immediate ontological unity of self and world but in the self's capacity for spontaneous separation from the world, which makes possible the constructive imposition of order on the chaos of sensibility.[70] In Schleiermacher's *Dialectic*, the mind's intellectual function is described as a spontaneous "will-to-know" that fashions the concepts that make the manifold objects of sensibility intelligible.[71] He describes the will as both this spontaneous desire[72] for knowledge and the intellectual judgments that guide the activity of practical reason.[73] Barth predictably conceives of freedom in entirely dogmatic terms. All "natural freedom," Barth says, is understood from the standpoint of faith, which knows that existence is ordered to the revelation of God in Jesus Christ. This claim means to Barth that the natural capacity for self-determination is rightly conceived only as the relational, positive affirmation of the covenant. Apart from the grace of the covenant, freedom is only bondage to a negative, self-seeking illusion.[74] Determined by that grace, it is true liberation.[75] The Word summons an ethical act of obedience or disobedience[76] that determines the "whole man."[77] It liberates the will's capacity to affirm the covenant, which is the reconciliation of created existence.[78] Only when Christ is the object of spontaneous self-determination is the human person willing in a way that is not bound by a disordered relation to God.[79]

This practical conception of grace as critical and social makes it impossible to subsume grace to creation. Their division is axiomatic for every aspect of this theology of grace. Its starting premise is the separation of the self from nature, which is the basis for the spontaneity that makes possible both the sinful alienation from reality and the gracious reconciliation with it. Grace is the concept that, when imposed on experience, rightly relates the separated subject to reality. But, where Catholic theology collapsed grace into creation, Schleiermacher and Barth understand grace as the domination of creation.[80] They repudiate metaphysics in favor of the critical relation to the world supplied by the social concept of grace. But, although both theologians believe they are pointing to the relational reality of grace, they have only succeeded in recasting that relation entirely in terms of the separation of subject and object. As Tillich noted with approval, the insistence that grace be conceived in terms of a social relation is transformed into the "principle" that that grace "stands beyond all its realizations."[81] The unrecognized consequence of that transposition is, ironically, that the social significance of grace is lost to the idea that the will's natural operation is spontaneous self-preservation. A unity of creation and grace founded on that separation, just like the Catholic union of immediate intuition, only secures their ontological separation and perpetuates the fragmentation of the existing social relation.

SELF-PRESERVATION, SOCIAL RELATION, AND REDEMPTION

Luther's critique of the scholastic doctrine of justification rejected its coupling of *caritas* with Aristotelian *habitus*. According to Luther, that union ran clearly against the grain of Paul's doctrine. What was taken to be the natural condition of the will's activity was instead the expression of a disordered relation to God and the world. Scholastic theologies of grace, and the medieval church in general, unintentionally reinforced this disordered relation. The church's recalcitrance regarding the critique only confirmed, for Luther, that its social relations were founded on the illusion of self-preservation and domination. According to Luther, the pursuit of self-interest and charity are mutually exclusive. Charity is by definition assuming the good of another as one's own. By refusing to recognize the discontinuity between a "natural" drive to self-preservation and the demands of charity, scholastic theology conceived of grace in a way that only reinforced the alienating power of sin.

Protestant theology critiqued this mistake by calling attention to the social rather than metaphysical character of grace. Acts of the will expressed the character of one's relation to God and the world. Broken relations produced sinful acts. Right relations made charitable acts possible. In this sense, grace is not so much understood as the gift that enables the will to fulfill its natural desire as it is the rightly ordered relation with God that is expressed in faith. The will is less the locus of self-determination than the medium through which the human relation with God is manifested. Calvin would emphasize much more than Luther the sociopolitical implications of this grace, which has led to much debate about the third use of the Law.[82] Yet, because Luther's *simul justus et peccator* is an empirical rather than a transcendental claim, it is best interpreted in the same terms that Gillian Rose understands Hegel's speculative proposition. It is not an attempt to argue for identity in the Christian between "sinner" and "justified" but a statement that calls attention to the experience of "the lack of identity between subject and predicate."[83] It is a statement that is meant to remind the sinning Christian that her faith is the expression of her right relation to God, and to remind the justified Christian that she sins. Out of this experience alone, Luther maintains, does the new possibility for the social reality of charity emerge.[84]

It is specifically because they were "speculative" doctrines in this sense that election and predestination for Luther and Calvin were not "metaphysical."[85] They were theological statements about the truth of the whole of reality, but they were made within the limitations of empirical experience. They insisted that the reality of faith was a true manifestation of God's eternal saving intention. Calvin's reason for reversing the order of predestination and providence was to underscore that time expresses God's saving purposes, as opposed to those purposes being subject to what happens in time. By the seventeenth century, however, orthodox Protestantism had begun to debate the order of salvation (*ordo salutis*) in which the divine decree came explicitly to be thought in ontological terms, as is the case with William Perkins's famous "Golden Chain."[86] In all three schools, the difference of grace from creation is mediated through their identity with God's eternal decree. Both creation and grace were distinct, contingent predicates of a single subject, the eternal decree.

The speculative logic of election in the Reformers, which made the empirical experience of nonidentity the necessary basis for any conception of unity between creation and grace, was reduced to a transcendental ontology of identity. Election was, for Luther and Calvin, a fluid and multivalent concept that ensured the confidence of faith within the failures and ambiguities of history. It could not be flattened out into a univocal identity. But for Protestant orthodoxy, by contrast, election was an ontological claim about the identity of God's act of creation with the act of grace. Schleiermacher and Barth constructed their doctrines of election in these ontological terms of identity. Though both critically differentiate grace from creation, they did not formulate the doctrine as an empirical account of the speculative experience of the nonidentity between grace and creation. They developed their doctrines of election as the theoretical concept in which the identity of creation and grace is known.

This ontological transposition of the doctrine of election had two important consequences. First, unlike Catholic theologies of intrinsic grace that begins with immediate intuition, this ontological inflection of the doctrine of election led Schleiermacher and Barth to make the separation of the subject from nature absolute. The empirical focus of the doctrine of election in Luther and Calvin meant that the same irreducibility of the individual to objectivity that made the Reformation critique possible was also subject to critique, in turn. It was on this basis that Luther could talk about the "natural" experience of the will's drive to self-preservation as a distortion of God's intention for it. Though we experience the will as "innately and inevitably" willing in this way did not mean simultaneously that the will possessed these qualities by nature.[87] But when the same experience of separation is ontologically conceived by Schleiermacher and Barth, it is constitutive of human selfhood and free agency. As they understand it, the sin lies not in the experience of separation but in the subject's existential relation to the reality of that separation. A free subject is ontologically distinguished from God and the world, and what matters is how that relation is conceptually determined, strictly as a division. A subject can produce alienation from its native capacity for self-determination only because its acts reinforce the contrast between itself and nature, which is self-preservation. Within the standpoint of faith, though, this same contrast can be known in its transcendental identity with God's election. In Schleiermacher, this means the subject rightly apprehends itself in an absolutely dependent relation to God. In Barth, it means that this capacity is liberated for the first time when it is taken up in obedience to the covenant partnership revealed in Jesus. The separation of the subject and nature is taken to be the ontological basis for spontaneous self-determination, and this spontaneity is the presupposition of the covenant relation between creation and God.

As a result, the scholastic view of the will's nature is revived in different terms, and Luther's important critique of its status as an illusion of a fragmented social relation is entirely lost. The idea of grace as a social relation is collapsed into the critical principle of differentiation that was originally derived from it. Entirely gone is the empirical emphasis on self-preservation as the expression of a fragmented, sinful social relation. The only social significance the critique retains is as a perpetual, ironic reassertion of the separation of the subject and nature. This is the "Protestant principle" of permanent revolution articulated by Tillich, a principle that disrupts all social realizations of grace's unity with creation.

For exactly the same reasons Luther critiqued scholastic theology, the union of grace and creation achieved by Schleiermacher and Barth in the doctrine of election is consequently an illusion. Their treatments of the doctrine elevate the separation of grace from creation to transcendental status. Although grace reconciles the subject with nature, it does so by dominating the manifold of experience. It imposes a concept on experience that draws its disparate elements into harmony. This union of subject and nature in grace is grasped in its harmony with the created order as a whole in the doctrine of election.

The unity in both doctrines is therefore achieved on the negative union of exclusion. It achieves unity by prohibiting those elements of experience that do not conform to the concept.[88]

Because it is negative, this union is also abstract. Barth's critique of Schleiermacher was correct, but his own solution only compounded the problem. By making Jesus Christ the electing God and elected human, Barth intended to eliminate all abstractness from the divine decree. Yet the objectivity Barth ascribed to the individual subject, Jesus, can be of universal significance only if his particularity is treated as archetypal, a universal structure of human consciousness.

In this respect, individuality for Schleiermacher and Barth is the constitutive exception to the whole. Both understand freedom in a way that is determined by bourgeois and liberal social relations. Faith, as Barth conceives it, is simply the alienated misrecognition of the practical activity of human creativity. The same is true, as Barth relentlessly demonstrated, about Schleiermacher. Any attempt to unite creation and grace in the critical concept will remain as abstract as in Catholic theologies of immediate intuition. That abstractness is the result of different causes. In Catholic theologies of grace, it is due to their lack of a critical and social concept of grace. In the case of Protestant theologies of grace, it is due to their collapsing of the social dimension of grace into a critical principle. Both attain a union that is only negative and abstract, which conceals its perpetuation of self-preservation and mediation of fragmented social relations.

In addition to the metaphysics of the will articulated in chapter 2, the union of creation and grace must also be a critical, social mediation. Barth lost sight of the fact that the second hypostasis of the Trinity is a relation, the social relation of Sonship. It is not a "person," in the Roman jurisprudential sense discussed in chapter 1. The Son is the relation begotten eternally from the Father. Jesus Christ is the historical, material, and temporal manifestation of that eternal relation in God. In Christ, Christians become participants in this eternal relation of Sonship.[89] Because our admission to that relation comes through the mediation of the person of Jesus, this relation is social. It is shared in the church, by the community of his disciples. A full articulation of the unity of grace and creation in these terms will demand coming to grips with the full social implications of our relation to God in Christ. We must find a way of affirming, in a nonabstract manner, the integrally ethical dimension of reality. This will require a metaphysics of the will and an affirmation of grace as a concrete social relation. Before making this argument, I will go directly to the sources of both the problem and its potential solution—namely, Augustine, Aquinas, and

Luther. The two trajectories of theology I have analyzed originally emerged from these three titans of theology, who currently stand in deadlock in the incoherent unity of creation and grace. By clearly recognizing the impasse, the resources for its resolution can also appear.

Notes

1. Ernst Troeltsch, *Protestantism and Progress: The Significance of Protestantism for the Rise of the Modern World*, trans. W. Montgomery (Philadelphia: Fortress Press, 1986), 34–40.

2. Paul Tillich, *The Protestant Era*, trans. James Luther Adams (Chicago: University of Chicago Press, 1948), 163.

3. Gerhard Ebeling, *Luther: An Introduction to His Thought*, trans. R. A. Wilson (Philadelphia: Fortress Press, 1970), 143. The Finnish interpretation is famously opposed to this interpretation of Luther's position, calling attention to his "ontological" advocacy of deification.

4. See Ibid., 156. See also the discussion of these differences specifically in terms of theological anthropology in Robert P. Scharlemann, *Thomas Aquinas and John Gerhard* (New Haven, CT: Yale University Press, 1964), 10–12 (especially n. 14). Scharlemann distinguishes between Aquinas's "formal-objectivist" and Gerhard's "dialectical-personalist" patterns of thinking. This is a consistent theme in the work of Emil Brunner. See especially *The Divine-Human Encounter* (London: SCM, 1944); *Truth as Encounter*, new ed. (Philadelphia: Westminster, 1964); *The Divine Imperative*, trans. Olive Wyon (Philadelphia: Westminster, 1947), 82–139; and Emil Brunner and Olive Wyon, *Revelation and Reason: The Christian Doctrine of Faith and Knowledge* (Philadelphia: Westminster, 1946), 362–74.

5. See Ebeling, *Luther*, which structures the treatment of Luther's theology according to such contrasts: "philosophy and theology," "the letter and the spirit," "the law and the gospel," etc.

6. On *caritas* and *habitus*, see Steven Ozment, "Luther and the Late Middle Ages: The Formation of Reformation Thought," in *Transition and Revolution: Problems and Issues of European Renaissance and Reformation History*, ed. Robert M. Kingdon (Minneapolis: Burgess, 1974), 109–29.

7. Ebeling, *Luther*, 157.

8. Note that this is not necessarily an "individual" relation in the now-pejorative sense.

9. This empahsis on the "substantial" consequences of this relation lies at the root of the Finnish emphasis on the role of *theosis* in Luther and is explicitly developed in opposition to the more "ethical" and nonmetaphysical reading of Luther developed by thinkers such as Ebeling. This reading will be discussed in chapter 5, but here it will suffice to note that I am in essential agreement with the Finnish interpretation but believe it has overlooked an important element of the more ethical reading of neo-Protestantism and has too hastily repudiated it.

10. See Tuomo Mannermaa, "Why is Luther So Fascinating? Modern Finnish Luther Research" in *Union with Christ: The New Finnish Interpretation of Luther*, eds. Carl E. Braaten and Robert W. Jenson (Grand Rapids: Eerdmans), 4–9.

11. Martin Luther, "Disputation against Scholastic Theology," in *Martin Luther's Basic Theological Writings*, ed. Timothy F. Lull (Minneapolis: Fortress Press, 1989), 34–39. A similar selection is given from Ozment in Peter A. Lillback, *The Binding of God: Calvin's Role in the Development of Covenant Theology* (Grand Rapids, MI: Baker, 2001), 64.

12. See Lillback, *Binding of God*, 58–80.

13. Luther's concern is to underscore that the will performs the good only by God's grace, an idea that is not about the will's nature but about the limitations of its self-determination. Apart from a proper relation to the God to whom the will is ultimately captive, the will's self-determination is only an expression of self-preservation and gratification (see theses 15 and 21 in

Martin Luther, "Heidelberg Disputation" in *Martin Luther's Basic Theological Writings*, ed. Timothy F. Lull (Minneapolis: Fortress Press, 1989), 47–61). Thesis 15 of the *Heidelburg Disputation*, written the following year (1518), states: "Nor could free will remain in a state of innocence, much less do good, in an active capacity, but only in its passive capacity." Thesis 16 continues: "The person who believes that he can obtain grace by doing what is in him adds sin to sin so that he becomes doubly guilty." Each of these claims is made against Scotus and Gabriel, both of whom developed a notion of the will's agency as fundamentally "indifferent" with regard to reason and "productive" with regard to its own self-movement. Recall the discussion in chapter 1 of Bernard J. F. Lonergan, *Verbum: Word and Idea in Aquinas*, ed. Frederick E. Crowe and Robert M. Doran, Collected Works of Bernard Lonergan 2 (Toronto: University of Toronto Press, 1988), 39n126.

14. Luther, "Disputation against Scholastic Theology," 30–33.

15. In this respect, Luther should be undrstood to anticipate Spinoza's claim that teleological ethics reverses the right order of ethical reasoning. See the appendix to book 1 in Baruch Spinoza, *The Essential Spinoza: Ethics and Related Writings*, trans. Samuel Shirley (Indianapolis: Hackett, 2006). The discussion of the will in Aquinas confirms that Luther does not wish to dispute this point; see chapter 4.

16. Luther, "Disputation against Scholastic Theology," 17.

17. Martin Luther, "Two Kinds of Righteousness," in *Martin Luther's Basic Theological Writings*, 159–60.

18. Ibid., 155–57.

19. Michael Root, "Schleiermacher as Innovator and Inheritor," cited in Matthias Göckel, *Barth and Schleiermacher on the Doctrine of Election: A Systematic-Theological Comparison* (New York: Oxford University Press, 2006), 18.

20. See Richard A. Muller, *Calvin and the Reformed Tradition: On the Work of Christ and the Order of Salvation* (Grand Rapids, MI: Baker, 2012), esp. 161–201.

21. My account of Protestant orthodox disputes about election is indebted to my reading of Richard A. Muller, *Christ and the Decree: Christology and Predestination in Reformed Theology from Calvin to Perkins* (Grand Rapids, MI: Baker, 2008), and to conversations with J. David Belcher. Particularly helpful was Belcher's unpublished research paper "The Christological Ground of Election: Arminius and Barth on Christ as Electing and Elected God," 2009; an earlier version was presented at the 44th annual meeting of the Wesleyan Theological Society, Anderson University, Anderson, Indiana, March 7, 2009. This essay is the only detailed engagement with the sources to demonstrate the commonality between Lutherans and Armenians that Barth notes in part 2 of *The Doctrine of God*, vol. 2 of *Church Dogmatics*, ed. G. W. Bromiley and T. F. Torrance, trans. G. W. Bromiley et al. (Edinburgh: T & T Clark,1957), henceforth cited as *CD* 2/2. Also, I refer specifically to Jacob Arminius here in order to acknowledge the important differences between late "Remonstrant" or "Arminian" theology and Arminius himself.

22. *De aet. Dei praed.* (1552), *Corpus reformatorum* 8:306–7, quoted in Barth, *CD* 2/2, 61.

23. Muller, *Christ and the Decree*, 1–75. Muller makes a basic distinction between Calvin's doctrine of election and those of his interpeters, a distinction that stands in tension with Barth's argument that Calvin's teaching remains abstract.

24. Some nuance is necessary on this point. Arminius's position undergoes development over the course of his writings, and the later Arminius may not precisely agree with the dominant Lutheran position. The later Arminius affirms an antecedent single predestination-election, grounded in Christ and his work of redemption, and this is the basis for a consequent double predestination of individuals. The antecedent and consequent will is part of the single, fourfold decree, as stated in Jacob Arminius, *Declaration of the Sentiments of Arminius* in *The Works of James Arminius*, trans. James Nichols (London: Longman, Hurst, Rees, Orme, Brown, & Green), 1:589–90: the decree that Jesus Christ will be "Mediator, Redeemer, Saviour, Priest and King" (which is a "general decree" in that it flows from God's antecedent love but is specific in that it is focused on Jesus Christ alone); the decree to receive those who repent, believe, and persevere; the decree to administer the means for repentance and belief; and the decree to save or

damn individuals, which is foreknowledge of those who would believe and persevere. The connection with Lutheranism, which Barth points to in *CD* 2/2, lies, as Belcher argues, in both the Lutherans' and Arminians' common appeal to Luis de Molina's *scientia media*, which intervenes between God's universal willing of salvation and the execution of the decree. There is a predestination to reprobation in Arminius, which is based on the divine "middle knowledge" future contingents. Arminius's use of the twofold love of God (*tweederley liefde Godes / duplex Dei amor*—antecedent/consequent love) corresponds to the Lutheran use of antecedent/consequent willing. On this point, I am relying on Belcher, "Christological Ground of Election."

25. Muller, *Christ and the Decree*, 19–22.

26. Barth, *CD* 2/2, 63–69.

27. Ibid., 63.

28. Ibid.; and Muller, *Christ and the Decree*, 10.

29. See Muller, *Christ and the Decree*, 10. The issue, for example, is not whether God first foresees future faith and subsequently elects, but whether knowledge of future faith is the logical basis for election or whether election alone is the basis of faith.

30. Heinrich Heppe, *Reformed Dogmatics Set Out and Illustrated from the Sources*, trans. G. T. Thomson (Grand Rapids, MI: Baker, 1950), 142.

31. My discussion of Schleiermacher's doctrine of election and its relationship to sin, absolute dependence, and ecclesiology is indebted to Göckel, *Barth and Schleiermacher*, esp. 16–103. Göckel's historical and textual work is convincing and informs the argument of my chapter. The reader is also directed to Bruce McCormack's discussion of the relationship between Barth's and Schleiermacher's doctrines of election in *Orthodox and Modern: Studies in the Theology of Karl Barth* (Grand Rapids, MI: Baker Academic, 2008), 21–88. The English edition of the *Dialectic* is only of the 1811 lectures: Friedrich Schleiermacher, *Dialectic; or, the Art of Doing Philosophy: A Study Edition of the 1811 Notes*, trans. Terrence N. Tice (Atlanta: Scholars, 1996). Henceforth, citations of this source appear in the text. I have also relied, throughout, on several important interpreters of Schleiermacher.

32. On this point, see Manfred Frank, "Metaphysical Foundations: A Look at Schleiermacher's *Dialectic*," in *The Cambridge Companion to Friedrich Schleiermacher*, trans. Jacqualine Mariña (Washington, DC: Catholic University Press), 15–34. See also Julia A. Lamm, "Reading Plato's Dialectics: Schleiermacher's Insistence on Dialectics as Dialogical," *Zeitschrift für Neuere Theologiegeschichte* 10, no. 1 (2003): 1–25.

33. Frank, "Metaphysical Foundations," 15.

34. Ibid.

35. On the role of proper thought in the *Dialectic* and its connection with Schleiermacher's introduction to *The Christian Faith*, trans. H. R. Mackintosh and J. S. Stewart, 2 vols. (New York: Harper & Row, 1963), I am indebted to John E. Thiel, *God and World in Schleiermacher's "Dialektik and Glaubenslehre": Criticism and the Methodology of Dogmatics* (Bern, Switz.: Lang, 1981). In my interpetation of the *Dialectic*, in addition to Thiel, I have followed Jack Forstman, *A Romantic Triangle: Schleiermacher and Early German Romanticism* (Missoula, MT: Scholars, 1977); and Frank, "Metaphysical Foundations"; and to Thandeka, *The Embodied Self: Friedrich Schleiermacher's Solution to Kant's Problem of the Empirical Self* (Albany: SUNY Press, 1995). The Platonic influence should also be noted; see Thiel, 14–17. See also Lamm, "Reading Plato's Dialectics." The Platonic influence is also discussed in Julia A. Lamm, "The Art of Interpreting Plato," in Mariña, *Cambridge Companion to Friedrich Schleiermacher*, 91–108. Thiel discusses the limits of speculation in the *Dialectic* in, *God and World*, 28–31. On the connection of Schleiermacher to Wittgenstein, see Andrew Bowie, "The Philosophical Significance of Schleiermacher's Hermeneutics," in Mariña, *Cambridge Companion to Schleiermacher*, 73–90.

36. I have here read Thiel's work on the connection between the *Dialectic* and *The Christian Faith*, together with Gockel's analysis of Schleiermacher's architecture of election. Also influential on the question of election has been the analysis of Schleiermacher's understanding of providence

and grace in Dawn DeVries and Brian Gerrish, "Providence and Grace: Schleiermacher on Justification and Election," in Mariña, *Cambridge Companion to Friedrich Schleiermacher*, 189–208. Equally influential is Brian A. Gerrish, "Nature and the Theater of Redemption: Schleiermacher on Christian Dogmatics and the Creation Story," *Ex Auditu* 3 (1987): 120–36.

37. See Thiel, *God and World*, 20.

38. See Thandeka, *Embodied Self*, 69.

39. Schleiermacher, *The Christian Faith*, 12–26.

40. Schleiermaker, quoted in Thandeka, *Embodied Self*, 114.

41. Gerhard Spiegler, *The Eternal Covenant: Schleiermacher's Experiment in Cultural Theology*, Makers of Modern Theology (New York: Harper & Row, 1967), especially 186–92. Spiegler's claim that Schleiermacher's exemption of God from relativity leads to the anthropological interpretation of his theology is bizarre, given that Spiegler's assertion appears to be grounded in a Hegelian conception of the Idea in dialectic that Schleiermacher is explicitly working against (ibid.). Furthermore, his claim overlooks the important role of the Redeemer in the inauguration of the Christian content of the feeling of absolute dependence.

42. Thiel notes that the 1828 lectures on the *Dialectic* achieve clarity on the God/world relation that is absent from the previous accounts when Schleiermacher arrives at the formula "The world is not without God, God is not without the world" (Die Welt nicht ohne Gott, Gott nicht ohne die Welt), in which "both ideas are not the same" (Beide Ideen sind nicht dasselbe) (*God and World*, 159). Thiel refers to this formula as a "cautelen" and argues that it is "a noetic correlation of God and world [that] is a philosophical construct that defines the nature of proper thinking itself" (160). These claims support Thiel's thesis that dogmatics, for Schleiermacher, is the articulation of the content of *Gefühl* within thought, specifically in terms of the regulative function exercised by a proper correlation of God and world in thought. His argument is convincing and has influenced my reading.

43. Schleiermaker, quoted in Thandeka, *Embodied Self*, 114.

44. See Thandeka, *Embodied Self*, 83–110. She notes that, in the 1831 lecture, Schleiermacher understands passive selfhood as that aspect in which "[w]e are given back to or return to ourselves as that which is being received." Her argument is that Schleiermacher is pointing to what remains of the self when neither thinking nor willing is occurring, to the "common border" of thought and will. The self "feels" itself in distinction from thought, which is a limit that is not also a thought. My interpretation of the significance of the realist implications of the feeling of absolute dependence is indebted to Thandeka's work on this point.

45. See ibid., 97. Thandeka notes that Schleiermacher is careful not to specify God here as the source of this feeling, because this would give a conceptual determination to the feeling that would destroy it.

46. On codetermination, see Schleiermacher, *Dialectic*, 39–47. See also Schleiermacher, *Christian Faith*, §4. See also Thandeka, *Embodied Self*, 101.

47. On the "whence" of feeling, see Schleiermacher, *Christian Faith*, §4.3–4.

48. See Thandeka, *Embodied Self*, 94–110.

49. See Jacqueline Mariña, *Transformation of the Self in the Thought of Friedrich Schleiermacher* (Oxford: Oxford University Press, 2008), 109–45. I will return to a discussion of this aspect of Mariña's work.

50. As Thiel has noted, though, the proper thinking developed in the *Dialectic* continues to structure the formulation of the role of *Gefühl* in dogmatics. Using the *Dialectic* as its guide for proper thought, Schleiermacher refers to the Christian church as the community that supplies discursive and intersubjective content to the otherwise immediate awareness of God-consciousness. See Thiel, *God and World*, 175.

51. See Schleiermacher, *Christian Faith*, §§30–31. On this way of relating the two parts, see Robert Sherman, *The Shift to Modernity: Christ and the Doctrine of Creation in the Theologies of Schleiermacher and Barth* (New York: T & T Clark, 2005). Sherman notes that Schleiermacher

designates three basic forms that dogmatic utterances can take: those that describe human "states of mind," those that present conceptions of the divine attributes, and those that present expressions regarding the nature of the world. The first is the most fundamental form, and it is presupposed by the other two (§30.2). This fact is at work in the system, where the first part of *The Christian Faith* describes the Christian religious self-consciousness in general, as it is considered apart from the antithesis of sin and grace, and the second part moves forward from that point, divided into the two aspects of sin and grace. Thus, Sherman notes that the system has nine distinct sections, with the doctrines explicated in each being correlated with the others. Sherman argues that this must be recognized in order to fully appreciate the interconnection between the treatments of doctrines. As Sherman insists, this entails that Schleiermacher's doctrine of creation is properly understood only in its relationship to all those propositions made throughout the system of the third form that relate to the nature and constitution of the world (Sherman, *Shift to Modernity*, 7.) The same point is also made well by Richard R. Niebuhr, "Christ, Nature, and Consciousness: Reflections on Schleiermacher in the Light of Barth's Early Criticisms," in *Barth and Schleiermacher: Beyond the Impasse?*, ed. James O. Duke and Robert F. Streetman (Philadelphia: Fortress Press, 1988), 28. In this regard, as Schleiermacher treats the doctrine of creation explicitly under the first form of human "states of mind" in the first part (§§40–41), this has important consequences in that it shows that this doctrine is not, for Schleiermacher, based upon a general account of the human experience of the world (or consciousness), but rather is rooted in the immediate experience of the particular consciousness of sin and grace that was brought about by the Redeemer. When this is further presented as falling under the general feeling of absolute dependence, it is because of the experience of the world that this redemption elicits that the Christian theologian extrapolates to claims about the nature of the world as a whole. As Sherman has noted, this entire procedure is explicitly christological for Schleiermacher: "[I]t is guided toward Christ from the very outset, and . . . its content must . . . be influenced by Christ as well, because of its 'genetic predisposition'" (*Shift to Modernity*, 29).

52. See Schleiermacher, *Christian Faith*, §§30–31. Subsequent citations of this source appear in the text. DeVries and Gerrish note that absolute dependence itself is a decidedly dogmatic category for Schleiermacher and not a general structure. This fact is expressed, they say, in the original creedal designation of God as "Pantocrator," which Schleiermacher understands as more fully expressing absolute dependence than any other Christian formulation. The absolute priority of God in the world's preservation is correlative with the doctrine of providence, which Schleiermacher understands as coincident with the traditional Reformed account of predestination. See *Christian Faith*, §36–41; and DeVries and Gerrish, "Providence and Grace," 190–91.

53. See Göckel, *Barth and Schleiermacher*, 99.

54. Göckel has not, discussed in detail the relationship of the *Dialectic* to the these questions. For this reason, I have read him together with Thiel. Particularly instructive is Göckel's note that Schleiermacher's discussion of creation and redemption in *The Christian Faith* is structured according to the argument of the 1819 essay "On the Doctrine of Election, Especially in Regard to the *Aphorisms* of Herr Dr. Bretschneider" (Göckel, *Barth and Schleiermacher*, 16n1). Göckel's helpful phrasing is this: "[T]he absolute causality of God is at once principally different from and equal in scope with the relative causality of the world" (99).

55. See Gerrish, "Nature and the Theater of Redemption," 196–216.

56. See also Göckel, *Barth and Schleiermacher*, 37–103.

57. This is the argument in Göckel, *Barth and Schleiermacher*

58. See also Gerrish, "Nature and the Theater of Redemption." As Göckel notes, because consciousness of this general truth of election is not itself generally apprehensible apart from its actualization in the life of the Redeemer and only as mediated by the Christian church, election is an essentially ecclesiological doctrine, insofar as it is ordered toward the realization of the kingdom of God. It is also divided between the reprobate and the elect insofar as the order of the whole involves some who do not participate, at any given time, in that decree. Although Schleiermacher insists on a single decree of election in God's preservation and governance of the world, that

decree is nonetheless received as differentiated according to the antithesis of sin and grace. Sin is not a reality for God, nor is it a general structure of consciousness. It is a specific determination of pious self-consciousness as communicated by the Redeemer, arising together with self-consciousness in contrast to the knowledge of his grace. More specifically, the social arrangement of the church that mediates this God-consciousness puts into relief the infirmity of all other social arrangements that do not have as their bases the propagation of the kingdom of God inaugurated by the Redeemer. See Göckel, *Barth and Schleiermacher*, 37–103.

59. See Göckel, *Barth and Schleiermacher*, 99.

60. See Terrence N. Tice, "Interviews with Karl Barth and Reflections on His Interpretations of Schleiermacher," in Duke and Streetman, *Barth and Schleiermacher*, 43–62.

61. Demonstration of this proximity between Schleiermacher and Barth is the overarching thesis of Göckel's work. Being convinced of his argument for the architecture of Schleiermacher's doctrine, I am also convinced by Göckel's reading of Barth and particularly his account of the development of Barth's doctrine of election. As with Schleiermacher, his work there regarding the relationship between the two thinkers and the development of Barth's own position on election is presupposed by my treatment of Barth here. See Göckel, *Barth and Schleiermacher*, 104–97.

62. *CD* 2/2, 60–81. Subsequent citations of this source will appear in this section of the text.

63. Karl Barth, "The Gift of Freedom: Foundation of Evangelical Ethics," in *The Humanity of God*, trans. John Newton Thomas and Thomas Wieser (Richmond, VA: John Knox, 1960), 76–81.

64. Karl Barth, part 1 of *The Doctrine of Creation*, vol. 3 of *Church Dogmatics*, ed. G. W. Bromiley and T. F. Torrance, trans. J. W. Edwards, O. Bussey, and H. Knight (Edinburgh: T & T Clark, 1958), 45; henceforth cited as *CD* 3/1 in the notes, with page numbers given parenthethically in this section of the text.

65. Barth distinguishes creation from grace while insisting on their continuity: "[T]he existence and being of the one loved are not identical with the fact that it is loved" (ibid., 97).

66. Göckel notes that *The Doctrine of Reconciliation* cannot be adequtely understood apart from grasping the importance of the revision of election in part 2 of *The Doctrine of God*. See *Barth and Schleiermacher*, 204.

67. Schleiermacher, *Christian Faith*, §62.

68. See Andrew Bowie, *Schelling and Modern European Philosophy: An Introduction* (New York: Routledge, 1994), 19–29.

69. See Joseph L. Mangina, *Karl Barth on the Christian Life: The Practical Knowledge of God*, Issues in Systematic Theology (New York: Lang, 2001). Despite the ways Mangina shows Barth working here against Cartesianism, he overlooks this basic assumption of Barth's, which is wholly Cartesian. This is no doubt tempered by his insistence that this all occurs within a relational and ethical order of obedience and/or rebellion. Yet it is simultaneously incited by his blatant reliance upon Hegelianism. See John Webster, *Barth's Ethics of Reconciliation* (Cambridge: Cambridge University Press, 1995), 229–30. See also Colin Gunton, "The Triune God and the Freedom of the Creature," in *Karl Barth: Centenary Essays*, ed. S.W. Sykes (Cambridge: Catholic University Press, 1989), 51.

70. Note that this is different from the assumption that the will is an infinite power in its own right, moving itself to its own operation.

71. See Schleiermacher, *Dialectic*, 24n34, 40, 63, 69. See Thandeka, *Embodied Self*, 63–92. What Schleiermacher is uncovering here is the way in which "pure thought" can be conceived of only as a "pure will" with no ability to produce what it intends: a distinct determinate thought. All such determinate thinking can be relatively conceived only insofar as it achieves its intentions on the basis of an activity it has received (Thandeka, 76–77.)

72. The relationship of this impulse to passivity is complex. On the matter, see Jacqueline Mariña, "Schleiermacher between Kant and Leibniz: Predication and Ontology," in *Schleiermacher and Whitehead: Open Systems in Dialogue*, ed. Christine Helmer (New York: de Gruyter, 2004),

73–91. See also Frank, "Metaphysical Foundations," 15–34. The connection of this idea to the Scotist understanding of will cannot be here traced. For this, see Vernon J. Bourke, *Will in Western Thought: An Historico-Critical Survey* (New York: Sheed & Ward, 1964), 84–89. Bourke notes the connection between Scotus, Ockham, Suarez, and Descartes. This is a clearly post-Cartesian notion, however, in that such willing is the active ground of determinate thinking, as opposed to being subsequent to intellectual thought, as in Scotus. This reflects the post-Suarezian influence and development of this idea carried out in Descartes. Note that the emphasis here is on the notion of "productivity." See Lonergan, *Verbum*, 39n126.

73. See the discussion of "dialogical dialectic" and "speculative dialectic" in Lamm, "Reading Plato's Dialectics."

74. This is the reason Barth understands anthropology in part 2 of *The Doctrine of Creation*, vol. 3 of *Church Dogmatics*, as an essentially christological doctrine. His designation of "real man" refers to the relationship between God and humanity as specified and actualized in Jesus Christ, who is the proper object for the specification of human willing. On this point, I am drawing on Joseph L. Mangina, *Karl Barth on the Christian Life: The Practical Knowledge of God*, Issues in Systematic Theology (New York: Lang, 2001). I am also indebted to Webster, *Barth's Ethics of Reconciliation*.

75. See Webster, *Barth's Ethics of Reconciliation*, 224–25. Webster notes that Barth's position implies that "moral selfhood is derived from, and intimately bound to, a source external to the self, and that the severing of that bond leads to incalculable moral losses" (225).

76. This is most clearly seen in *CD* 1/1, 201, quoted in Mangina, *Karl Barth on the Christian Life*, 37: "If God's Word is not spoken to animals, plants and stones but to men, and if determination by God's Word is really a determination of human existence, in what, then, will it consist if not in the fact that the self-determination in which man is man finds its absolute superior in determination by God, that as self-determination, and without in the least being affected or even destroyed altogether as such, *it receives a direction, is set under a judgment and has impressed upon it a character, in short, it is determined in the way that a self-determining being is by a word and that man is by the Word of God*" (my emphasis).

77. The event of the Word of God provides cognitive, intellectual determination for the relative—but no less fundamental—capacity for self-determination that characterizes human being. Mangina notes the three basic corollaries that Barth draws from this, namely, that it frees us to affirm that all areas of life are open to determination by God, that all facets of the human person are engaged in that determination, and that no special aspect of the human person is privileged in that determination (*Karl Barth on the Christian Life*, 38).

78. Ibid., 36. Colin Gunton has made this same point, noting its real significance in his discussion of *CD* 2/2. He notes the intimate connection between God's Trinitarian self-determination in election, which corresponds to the election of God's people. The love and freedom that define the being of God in election have their counterpart in the love and freedom of the creature, which is liberated in its determination by, in, and through God's election. Such liberated freedom is our self-determining "election" of God, which is also said to be our "autonomy." This is a kind of self-determination that corresponds to God's election itself inasmuch as it is personal, thereby requiring a certain free self-determination in relation to this object, namely, "responsibility . . . decision . . . obedience . . . action." *CD* 3/2, 511, quoted in Gunton, "Triune God," 51.

79. See Mangina, *Karl Barth on the Christian Life*, 35. See also 32–45. As Mangina underscores, Barth's point is that it is with the actually existing human being as addressed by the Word that theological anthropology is concerned. This is the basis for his insistence that knowledge of the reality of God's Word becomes possible only in the event of revelation itself (35).

80. See Gillian Rose, *Hegel contra Sociology* (New York: Verso, 2009), 71–77.

81. Paul Tillich, *The Protestant Era*, 163.

82. See Bernard Lohse, *Martin Luther's Theology: Its Historical and Systematic Development*, trans. Roy A. Harrisville (Minneapolis: Fortress Press, 1999), 191–92 and 270–76.

83. Rose, *Hegel contra Sociology*, 52.

84. See Luther, "Two Kinds of Righteousness," 157–64.

85. See Rose on Hegel's "speculative proposition," in *Hegel contra Sociology*, 51–53.

86. Muller, *Calvin and the Reformed Tradition*, 161–201.

87. Note that I am here stating the inverse consequence of Luther's claim that though the will "innately and inevitably" does evil, this does not mean that the will is evil by nature. Luther's premise is that an act of self-preservation is an evil act because it by definition excludes an act of charity.

88. See Rose, *Hegel Contra Sociology*, 209–17.

89. For this insight into eternal Sonship (though not as a critique of Barth), I am indebted to Sarah Coakley, "Why Three? Some Further Reflections on the Origins of the Doctrine of the Trinity," in *The Making and Remaking of Christian Doctrine: Essays in Honour of Maurice Wiles*, eds. Sarah Coakley and David Pailin (Oxford: Clarendon Press, 1993), 29–56; see also Mark A. McIntosh, *Divine Teaching: An Introduction to Christian Theology* (Oxford: Blackwell, 2007), 111–38.

4

Metaphysics and Social Relations
Creation and Grace in Augustine, Aquinas, and Luther

Never mistake motion for action.
—ERNEST HEMINGWAY TO AVA
GARDNER

In the first chapter of this study, I argued that the separation of the subject from nature in modern philosophy raised a particularly acute problem for theology. That division seemed to eliminate any possibility for certain knowledge of God. The unity of the doctrines of creation and grace became the theological focus for addressing the difficulties raised by this separation. The previous two chapters analyzed the contemporary Catholic and Protestant attempts to reclaim that unity. In both cases, the achieved union is illusory, because it is abstract and negative, which serves only to perpetuate the separation. In its own way, each fails to recognize the division as the expression of an actually existing social fragmentation and to conceive the union of grace and creation as a social relation. I concluded chapter 3 suggesting that my analysis points to a demand to recuperate metaphysics from Catholic theology in a way that fully integrates the critical emphasis in Protestantism on the social location of grace, which is achieved in its doctrines of justification and election. That synthesis will entail retrieving the significance for contemporary theology of Aquinas's metaphysics of the will and the Reformers' emphasis on social relations. Right understanding of the will and social relations, of course, are two interconnected aspects of actually existing ethical life, which is obscured by the fragmented (abstract and negative) bourgeois relations that condition our present thought about social reality.

The present chapter explores the historical sources of the patterns of thought in theology that now reinforce the fragmentation of this order and reproduce its illusions. This first part identifies, in the relation between Augustine's metaphysics of creation to his mature theology of grace, the source of the mistakes in the Catholic and Protestant trajectories, as well as the resources for a solution. I show that the metaphysical incoherence of Augustine's theologies of creation and grace is caused not by a foolish embrace of election but by his dependence on the flawed account of the will in his early ontology of participation. That flaw prevents him from uniting the metaphysics of creation with his insight into grace as a social relation. Lacking a coherent account of the will, every attempt to integrate the social with the metaphysical reduces their relation to one of ontological identity, which establishes a double bind between the affirmations of God's immutability and human freedom. Two conflicting possibilities remain: one ordered to the metaphysical subsuming of grace to creation, and the other emphasizing a social relation in which grace dominates creation. Substantiating these claims will involve analyzing Augustine's genetic development in the light of present historical scholarship.[1]

The second part of the chapter traces the decisive corrections in the two trajectories made by Aquinas and Luther. Aquinas corrects Augustine's metaphysical errors about divine immutability and the will, whereas Luther recognizes and develops the critical moment internal to the social concept of grace. I will show that both Aquinas and Luther pressed toward a metaphysics of social relation that neither could finally sustain. In each case, the social relation is dissolved into ontological identity, an abstract and negative unity of creation and grace.

THE METAPHYSICS OF CREATION

CREATIO EX NIHILO: IMMUTABILITY, GOODNESS, AND SELF-DETERMINATION

Gerhard May has shown that the basic outline for the doctrine of *creatio ex nihilo* first appeared in the work of Basilides in the second century as an attempt to unite the highest god of Gnosticism with the sovereign God of the Hebrews.[2] Basilides wanted to appropriate the gnostic idea of the "world-seed" and link it directly to a single divine act.[3] His synthesis of Hellenistic metaphysics and Hebraic Scripture was further developed a generation later in apologetic writings of Irenaeus, Tatian, and Tertullian.[4] But it was Augustine who realized the full implications of this affirmation by drawing together its various themes into a single whole.

In his early anti-Manichean writings, Augustine developed a complete philosophical account of *creatio ex nihilo*, which set it in opposition to all metaphysical dualisms.[5] Although Augustine's rejection of dualism would become central to the Western tradition's appropriation of his argument, it is the logic of his position that would have the greatest impact on subsequent developments in his theology of grace.[6] In particular, the convertible relation between immutability and goodness in his argument often goes unrecognized.[7] Augustine's affirmation of that convertibility led him to establish a grammar for divine sovereignty, expressed principally in *creatio ex nihilo*, the implications of which he only gradually came to realize in the context of working out his mature theology of grace.[8]

Most accounts of Augustine's argument against Manichaeanism focus on his repudiation of its doctrine of an essential evil materiality. For Manichaeanism, God and matter were antitheses. The essential passivity of matter, which made it mutable, corruptible, and subject to suffering, was absolutely contrasted with God's immutable self-determination. Human souls had fallen from heaven and become ensnared in matter, but a spark of their divine origin remained in them. Salvation, for Manichaeism, meant the liberation of this divine spark, turning away from the corruption of diversified matter and returning to unity with the immutable stability of God.[9] In modified form, each of these ideas remained a constitutive aspect of Augustine's early theology of both creation and grace until about 417 ce.[10] Yet, under the influence of Ambrose's Neoplatonism, which most likely drew heavily from Origen, Augustine repudiated the Manichaean doctrine of evil matter. He developed his argument against Manichaeanism, specifically as a more consistent application of the idea of divine immutability that he otherwise shared with them.

Augustine's debate with Fortunatus is the best example of turning the Manichaeans' understanding of God's immutable self-determination against them.[11] Probing the Manichaean rationale for the soul's descent into matter, Augustine presses Fortunatus as to whether it is his assumption that this occurred in order to spare God injury. Fortunatus responds that, as absolute and immutable, God has no need of protection from injury, but that the soul was sent to inhabit the material nature in order to restrain and delimit it. Augustine then replies that, if that nature is truly contrary to God and in need of limitation, then Fortunatus unwittingly believes God is passable and subject to necessity. He thinks of God as existing in a dialectical relation of mutual determination with materiality.[12] And with two opposed metaphysical principles, it is only the arbitrary contingency of fate that is taken to be absolute. A consistent appeal to

God's absolute immutability demands not its contrast with materiality but the affirmation that matter is God's creation, absolutely dependent on God for its existence.

Because God's goodness and immutability are convertible, matter participates in the divine Good.[13] As Schleiermacher put it, the Source of the immanent contrasts of material reality has no contrast itself. Either all things are determined by God or all things (including God) are subject to fate and their goodness is vitiated.[14] The convertibility of the divine immutability and goodness points directly to creation out of nothing.[15] Mutable matter must be understood as a relative expression of God's absoluteness, grounded in and governed by God.[16] In this respect, matter has a positive existence that evil entirely lacks.[17] God does not send the soul into matter in order to limit its evil, but the soul is rather persuaded to turn away from God by its own free choice and to embrace the unintelligibility of evil.[18]

With his metaphysics of creation grounded so firmly in God's immutability and its convertibility with goodness, the decisive question for Augustine would prove to be whether the absolute sovereignty his argument demands could be sustained within his Neoplatonic scheme. The challenge to his assumptions would first appear in this theology of grace in relation to the soul's capacity for self-determination and the nature of its relation to God.

THE WILL

The argument for creation out of nothing from the start made volitional intent a key theme of Augustine's theology.[19] The anti-Manichaean writings show the early importance Augustine placed on choice in the doctrine of creation out of nothing, and book 7 of *Confessions* identifies his insight into volitional intent as decisive for his break from an implicitly materialist metaphysics.[20] Writings of the Donatist and Pelagian controversies, however, brought into relief the specifically social significance of grace. The anti-Donatist writings made it clear that Augustine understood the presence of grace to be directly expressed in the social relations of the church. Sacramental validity is determined not by the maintenance of ritual purity but by the use (*usus*) to which worldly material (*res*) is put. That use expresses the reality intended by the participants.[21] Valid sacraments manifest the reality of the church's charitable social relations, which Donatist sacraments do not share.[22] The anti-Pelagian writings further reinforce this point by showing that the will aims at the social virtue of justice, which is perfected in charity. The exercise of charity, however, requires the presence of God's love, which converts the desire for self-preservation into the self-giving love for God. And this same notion of voluntary intention (*intentio voluntatis*) is directly linked to the Holy Spirit in *The Trinity*, where its function in the mind is to unify the diverse elements of experience to their goal.[23]

James Wetzel points to a passage in *On Two Souls*, which reiterates Augustine's opposition to Manichaean fatalism and appeals to the central role played by the divine will in the doctrine of creation: "[In the Manichaean system,] there is no judgment on the basis of merits and no providence, and the world is governed—or rather not governed—by chance rather than by reason. Governance, after all, should not be attributed to chance."[24] In addition to Wetzel, Albrecht Dihle, Charles Kahn, and Richard Sorabji have each argued (though offering slightly different rationales) that Augustine is responsible for inventing the idea of the will as a psychological operation distinct from desire and the intellect.[25] They argue that Augustine clearly, in Wetzel's words, distinguished between "what happens by nature and what happens by will" in a way that makes the first "clearly delineated concept of the voluntary."[26] Sorabji argues that the uniqueness of this idea is due to Augustine's particular use of a variety of concepts he had acquired from others, none of which did the same work as Augustine's "will."[27] Most notably, the link Augustine drew between creation and God's goodness led him to understand the natural world as a communication of God's personal, ethical agency, an agency to which personal, human agents were summoned to cooperate.[28]

The social emphasis of volition was implicitly present in Augustine's theology of creation from the start. Though it was instrumental for his break with Manichaeanism, however, it remained essentially Neoplatonic.[29] As Vernon Bourke showed, the discussion of the will in book 10 of the *Confessions* essentially repeats the concept of volition set out in Plotinus's *Ennead* 6. Robert O'Connell has also noted the important role *Ennead* 6 played in Augustine's argument for divine omnipresence.[30] Bourke specifically notes the link between the will and omnipresence in the One, which is radically "diffusive of itself and thus constitutive of at least one aspect of the many things of this universe." The One is not "an agent of the process of world-making" but "an exemplary cause, and not the only one, in the process."[31] The world is the necessary excess of the One's perfect act of absolute self-determination: "In the One, power (*dynamis*) is not open to contraries; it is an irresistible and immovable force, which is the greatest possible. . . . Who could change it, since it is generated from the divine will, and is His will (*boulesin ousan*) itself? . . . Will was, then, in His essence; in fact, it (*boulesis*) is nothing other than His essence. . . . He is entirely will; there is nothing in Him that does not will."[32] Plotinus rejects any dialectical contrast to the One on grounds that its "power" (*dynamis*) determines all that follows from it. The One is absolute because the ideal and the real perfectly correspond in its "self-making."[33] All finite willing participates in the primordial self-constitution of the One: "All was will. . . . There is then nothing before that will: God and will were primally identical."[34]

The same idea of immutable self-determination is given in Augustine's *The Catholic Way of Life and the Manichean Way of Life*:

> For that exists in the highest sense of the word which continues *always the same, which is throughout like itself, which cannot be corrupted or changed, which is not subject to time, which admits no variation* in its present as compared to its former condition. This is existence in its true sense. For in this signification of the word existence there is implied a nature which is self-contained, and which continues immutably. Such things can be said only of God, to whom there is nothing contrary. . . . For the contrary of existence is non-existence.[35]

Divine simplicity is that which "immutably" continues in a "self-contained" state with "no variation in its present as compared to . . . former condition."[36] God's immutability is a perfect correspondence of the ideal with the real, a perfect act of absolute self-determination. In these early Neoplatonic invocations of the divine will, Augustine is unable to make the subtle distinction that Aquinas will later make in recognizing God as the act of existence (*esse*) rather than as a perfect and immutable act of self-determination.

In this Neoplatonic ontology, human willing participates in God's absolute self-determination. In *On Free Choice*, for example, Augustine's argument against an evil materiality is based on the assertion that the human will alone is responsible for its good or evil acts. Through its intention (*intentio*), a soul either draws the diverse elements of finite existence into a coherent relation to their Absolute Source or becomes ensnared in the distention (*distentio*) and turmoil of the mutable materiality.[37] When it is preoccupied only with the diversity of materiality, the soul lacks any ultimate object of reference that is capable of rightly ordering and integrating its divided desires.[38] But by turning the mind to the highest Good and the Source of all, all objects and desires are united and rightly related.[39] Conceived this way, the early Augustine understood the will as the soul's innate capacity to give intellectual determination to its desire.[40] This intellectualist emphasis apparent in Augustine's earliest definition of the will, given in *On Two Souls*, which appears to depend on Plato's definition of the soul as the capacity for self-movement. The will, Augustine says, is "a movement of the soul, with nothing forcing it either not to lose something or to acquire something."[41]

As Risto Saarinen has argued, although this definition of the will makes the important distinction of volitional from natural action, it does not distinguish the will from the intellect.[42] Willing is, in fact, here considered entirely in terms of the intellectual direction of desire, or what Aquinas calls in the *Prima pars* an "intellectual appetite." As a result, Augustine's early doctrine of creation is built on an understanding of the will that explains "actions performed against better judgment [sin] . . . in terms of ignorance."[43] The fall of the soul and its entanglement with matter are caused by ignorance and illusion, and can be thus corrected with the proper unifying object.[44] It is only later, when Augustine recognizes that the internal conflict described by Paul in Romans 7 (and by himself in *Confessions* 8)[45] cannot be explained by ignorance alone, that Augustine began to perceive the social determination of the will and to distinguish it from the intellect.[46]

That distinction was clearly made by the time Augustine wrote *Retractions*. That text reiterates the early definition of the will from *Two Souls* but glosses it to include his recognition of the importance of social relations, which he learned during the twenty years of controversies that followed his letter to Simplician (396–417 ce).[47] No longer is defective willing simply a matter of ignorance. It is a matter of justice: for "the will to retain or to acquire what justice forbids and from which one is free to hold back."[48] Augustine's engagement with the Donatist and Pelagian controversies by this time had taught him that this justice is identical to charity. In other words, defective willing is self-preserving—seeking "to retain or acquire what justice forbids" and from which one can "hold back"—rather than charitable. And charity is a possibility only on the prior condition of the presence of God's love, which restores the right relation with God that is shared in the church's common life.[49] In these terms, a will is "free" only when it shares, with God and others, in the social relation of charity.[50]

With his doctrine of creation, Augustine established the terms on which the world would be understood not as an emanation from the One but an intentional object of God's divine will, participating in God's goodness and providence. In doing so, he also opened the door within a Neoplatonic metaphysics to the idea that the world exists in an absolutely dependent, but nonetheless social, relation with God. This meant that not only does material reality not exist in contradiction to the reality of God's goodness but also it can be understood as a gratuitous and positive reality in its own right, distinct from and in dynamic relation with God.[51] His critique of metaphysical dualism linked the objective goodness of the world directly to the absoluteness of God's self-determination and the possible failure of humanity's. The argument elegantly removed the ontological possibility of evil and did so by implicitly shifting the register of evil into the ethical domain of social relations. Sin was the expression of a broken relation with God, a failure not just to will the good but also in the will's relation to it.[52]

But this also created a problem. The metaphysics of creation understood its goodness to depend on the perfection of God's self-determination and the failure of humanity's. As long as failures in willing could be explained as ignorance, the immediate coincidence of social and ontological goodness was maintained. But once Augustine recognizes that the theology of grace demands greater precision in distinguishing the will from the intellect, the increased emphasis on social relation that results brings into relief the competition between divine and human self-willing that was implicit in the Neoplatonic metaphysics in which his early theology of creation was framed. If God's immutability is defined as a perfect act of absolute self-determination as it was in the early theology of creation, then preserving the world's objective goodness in his mature theology of grace would appear to require God's will to dominate the human will. Yet, simultaneously, Augustine had opened the door to the realization that, because it is God's creation, an object of the divine will, the world exists in a truly positive, social relation with God.[53]

GRACE AS A SOCIAL RELATION

You are my choice, and only by your gift
can I please either you or myself.
—AUGUSTINE, *CONFESSIONS*

Augustine's treatment of grace and freedom has been, from the beginning, an almost perpetual concern for philosophers, theologians, and historians. Because of this, it is surprising that so little attention has been given to the relationship between his theology of grace and his theology of creation. It is all the more puzzling given the important place of free choice (*liberum arbitrium*) in his metaphysics of creation.[54] From the time of writing *On Free Choice* (388–95 ce) to 413 ce, Augustine's dominant understanding of the relationship of grace to the will was that of Platonic spiritualism.[55] Grace is God's assistance in doing the good necessary for salvation, and that assistance is given in the form of intellectual illumination. The eternal Word immediately communicates to the soul the laws that govern creation, and these are the principles that direct the soul to God.[56] A soul that is turned away from God is darkened and lacks the insight necessary to do the good. But when a soul turns toward God, the good is once more illuminated and the good can be done. It is Jesus Christ who perfectly illuminates the good, giving the complete and final knowledge of God that overcomes the illusions of sin. His continued presence in the church gives the assistance necessary for good performance, and his incarnation and resurrection give assurance of the final triumph over death.[57]

It is clear that during the years following the writing of *On Free Choice*, Augustine began to wrestle considerably with Paul's doctrine of grace, specifically his paradigmatic text on election, Romans 9–11. In his letter to Simplician, Augustine made a decisive transition, commenting on Romans 9:16 ("[I]t depends not on human will or exertion but on God who shows mercy") and 9:11-12 ("[e]ven before they had been born or had done good or bad").[58] This passage made clear to him that the Platonic spiritualism in which his theology of grace was framed allowed for the possibility of meriting salvation and avoiding divine punishment apart from Christ and outside the church,[59] and he rejected this possibility as contradicting Paul's teaching that all share in the guilt of Adam's sin.[60] Because of this, all right knowledge and good action must be possible only on the basis of God's prior grace.[61]

As *Confessions* dramatizes, Augustine's reading of Romans 7 alerted him to the internal conflict within the will that knows the good and seeks to do it apart from grace.[62] He now understood grace according to his interpretation of Paul's reading of the Law. Within the conditions of sin, no possibility of doing good exists, because all available choices are sinful. The Law gives the knowledge necessary for salvation, but that knowledge only reveals the incapacity of the will to do it.[63] In this way, Augustine recognizes the difference between implicitly desiring a good object, knowing the truth of its goodness, and explicitly willing it as a good object.[64] When the gospel finally arrives, however, the futility of this state is known for the first time in the light of the forgiveness for failures won by Christ and the gift of the Holy Spirit, in whom the will is moved to love God above all else and the neighbor as oneself.[65]

In writing *To Simplician*, Augustine became aware of the importance not just of the gift of grace prior to human willing but also of the context that determines all human willing. In order to harmonize his new theology of grace with his earlier metaphysics of free choice, Augustine developed the argument that God orchestrates the conditions, suited to the elected individual's character and heart, in which to give the most attractive presentation of the gospel, ensure a positive response, and preserve her capacity for self-determination.[66] Though Augustine now realized that knowledge of the good alone was not sufficient for its performance and accepted the social context of the will's exercise, he still assumed that under the right conditions knowing the good would result in its freely being chosen. As Burns points out, his model remained one of persuasion, which simply sidesteps the major challenge posed by Romans 9:11-12—a passage not about conversion but about God's decree in favor of one brother and against another prior to their birth.[67]

Between 396 and 417 ce, as I noted earlier, Augustine's understanding of the social context and determination of the will's operation was refined by his engagements with the Donatist and Pelagian controversies.[68] The mark of sin, for Augustine, is shown in the conflict within the self over the good it knows and its inability to do it. The Holy Spirit, which is the presence of God's own love in the soul, bestows the charity that brings the diffuse desires of the self into harmony with the dictates of justice by ordering them properly to God. During these controversies he recognized that, apart from the gift of charity given by the Holy Spirit, the natural capacity for self-determination remains simply an expression of self-preservation, which is inimical to charity. His consistent charge against the Donatists is that their preoccupation with ritual and ecclesial purity, even if it were correct, would be nothing more than the sinful drive to self-preservation and not charity.[69] The true sacramental life of the church is expressed in the charitable social relations of unity, which are the setting for the reception of grace. For the Donatists, by contrast, the love of God and neighbor is subordinated to self-constitution, a negative contrast to their own ritual purity. Augustine applied the same idea to the Pelagian insistence on the inviolability of the capacity for free choice. He pointed to the contradiction between the commandment to love God for God's own sake and loving God for salvation. The attempt to fulfill the commandment results in a performative violation of it, which treats God as a means to self-preservation rather than an end to be loved for itself alone. Both of these controversies expanded Augustine's insight into the social location of the will, its determination within a social context, and the constructive or destructive social implications of that determination.[70] Consequently, after the Donatist controversy and continuing through the Pelagian dispute, Augustine ascribed the entirety of redemption to God alone.[71] From the giving of the call to its acceptance, and perseverance in it—each moment is henceforth understood to be determined solely by God's eternal election.[72] Nonetheless, throughout the controversies of these years, Augustine continued to maintain that God's grace did not violate human self-determination.[73]

But beginning in 413 ce, Augustine was led to repudiate explicitly the Origenist theory that the soul had sinned in a prior spiritual state and subsequently fallen into the body.[74] Robert O'Connell has argued that this is important evidence that Augustine adhered to the theory of the soul was first created in an immaterial state as late as 418.[75] Regardless of the merits of that argument, what is clear is that the reasons Augustine gives for rejecting the idea also apply in a fundamental way to his prior understanding of self-determination. If salvation finally depends simply on God's persuasion of our spontaneous self-determination, then this grace is not sufficient to ensure we will not fall again. It is only here that Augustine directly confronts for the first time the full implications of God's election in Romans 9:11-12. From this point forward, he concedes that God's election to salvation occurs prior to all acts and merits, prior even to the existence of the elect individuals.

From this standpoint, Augustine considers sin entirely in terms of a broken relation. It is not the result of a turning away from the one immutable and spiritual good to the multiple changeable goods of matter. Sin originates in Adam and Eve's spontaneous self-preserving pride (*superbia*), which is the rupture of right relation with God that is expressed and disclosed in their act of disobedience. Consequently, Augustine no longer maintains that God's grace appeals to the soul's capacity for self-determination, but instead that grace entirely transforms the will's evil orientation, literally producing the willing and acting of conversion. This willing and acting is the work of the Holy Spirit in Christians, and it is sufficient both to ensure perseverance in faith throughout this life and to secure salvation in eternity.

Augustine's greatest challenge from this point on was in resolving the conflict between God's action and human self-determination.[76] Augustine's earliest rejection of dualism had been implicitly bound up with ethics. The objective goodness of the world was linked to the immutability of the divine willing, while evil was the result entirely of the failure of the human will. However, his shift away from a metaphysics of self-determination and toward the prior rectitude of relation elevated the social relation to a higher place in his theology, while appearing to vitiate human willing altogether.

Nevertheless, election brings an increased emphasis on the social location of the will. Justice and relational rectitude are from this point on central to Augustine's theology of grace. The central place of social relations in grace is displayed in the center of Augustine's mature theology of grace. Their importance to his later thought is displayed in the title he gave to his most sustained and comprehensive presentation of the union of grace and creation, *City of God*. By that time, Augustine had come to repudiate self-determination as the self-preserving drive to domination that gives rise to the City of Humanity.[77] Yet Augustine still conceived this greater emphasis on social relations in the doctrine of election in terms of Neoplatonic metaphyiscs even after 417 ce. This metaphysics, however, was now in direct conflict with the social terms of his mature theology of grace. This conflict is apparent on two fronts.

First, his mature theology of grace fractured the metaphysics of ontological participation. His debate with Fortunatus showed that the Manichaean idea that God exiled the soul to the body to restrain material evil rested on an assumption that violated God's immutability. Echoing Plotinus, Augustine argued that material reality participates in God's goodness, and the soul turns away from God and falls of its own free choice. But upon recognizing that ignorance was insufficient to explain failures to will the good, Augustine could no longer presume that grace was universally available and immediately coincident with creation. Grace must instead be a special divine act related more closely to the social setting of the will's exercise than to the intellectual illumination of being. This same realization also brought into clear relief for the first time the social implications implicit in his doctrine of creation. Creation out of nothing was not simply a superior metaphysics of the absolute; it was also an intersubjective social relation between agencies.

Second, the development of these parallel distinctions between intellect/will and creation/grace destabilized Augustine's elegant unity of divine immutability and goodness. Human willing could no longer simplistically be understood as mutable participation in God's immutable self-determination. The superior divine initiative of grace, now distinct from creation, must precede and condition all human willing of the good. Ordered according to God's eternal decree of election, grace could only be conceived, in the metaphysics of ontological participation, as God's domination of natural creation. Augustine understands even the natural goodness of creation, in this light, as the transcendent law of order imposed by God on reality.[78] His meditations in *City of God* on the world's darkness and light, which reflect the activity of fallen and beatified angels, well illustrate the shift in his thinking from *On Free Choice*.[79] The same stress on the social conception of God's sovereignty is likewise apparent throughout his latest anti-Pelagian writings.

Prior to *City of God*, in his *Literal Commentary on Genesis*, Augustine had attempted to conceive of God's governance of particulars in terms of the Platonic category of abstract form. Anticipating many of the ontological elements of later Protestant orthodoxy, Augustine argued that the forms of individual particulars exist eternally in the divine mind and are temporally realized in history.[80] God governs these particulars through the general principles of measure, number, and weight that order the growth, development, and decay of material reality.[81] "Seeds" (*rationes seminales*) of the divine ideas, like the Stoic *logoi spermatikoi*, are implanted in creation.[82] As with Basilides, "the whole cosmic process develops according to the original plan of God," with the seeds of these immanent rational principles serving as the instruments of God's government and election.[83] Nonetheless, because these rational principles are abstract, they do not violate the human soul's capacity for self-determination. Rather, they are the basis for God's intrinsic orchestration of salvation history to ensure the elect's free acceptance of the call to conversion. In this way, the rational principles were the means by which Augustine sought to incorporate his theology of grace into the metaphysics of immediate unity demanded by ontological participation. But by the time he completed *City of God* (426–427 ce), a decade later, Augustine had completely rethought creation as an ontology of the divine decree.

The significance of both the *Literal Commentary on Genesis* and *City of God* is that they clearly show Augustine reconceiving his early doctrine of creation in the light of his mature theology of grace. And these two different accounts of unity anticipate the problems I have identified in Catholic (immediate intuition) and Protestant (conceptual mediation) theologies of grace, which reduce its relation to creation to ontological identity. The competition between divine immutability that results from this reduction is due to the continued influence of the Neoplatonic ontology of participation, which did not allow for the discrete operational integrity of creatures, who were simply finite expressions of God's absolute freedom. Once Augustine distinguished grace from creation, he could sustain the divine immutability and the world's goodness, only if God's freedom subjugated human freedom, and if God's grace dominated creation. The metaphysical scheme did not have the resources for sustaining the decisive difference between creation and grace or intellect and will without reducing them to an abstract ontological identity.

It was in this way that Augustine established the theological bases for both the immediate subsuming of grace to creation (Catholic) and the mediated domination of creation by grace (Protestant). Because of Augustine's unparalleled authority in the theologies of creation and grace, these two rival trajectories would remain endemic and incommensurable within Western theology. In the final section of this chapter, I will examine the developments within these two paths.

Nature and the Supernatural: Aquinas on the Metaphysics of the Will

> *The imperfect is always for something more perfect: therefore, just as matter is for form, so also form, which is first act, is for its operation, which is second act; and so operation is the end of a created thing.*
>
> –Thomas Aquinas, *Summa Theologiae*

De Lubac and Rahner directly confronted the problem of the continued division of grace and creation in Western theology, but they lost sight of the central place of the will in that legacy. As I have shown, the distinction of the will from the intellect is essential to the work of Augustine and Aquinas. In Augustine, it disrupted the ontology of participation that was the backbone of his early theology of creation while simultaneously revealing the implicit social dimension of both creation and grace. In Aquinas, the distinction of will and intellect was integral to the differentiation of the supernatural from the natural. Both de Lubac and Rahner reverted to the Platonic notion of the will that Augustine and Aquinas abandoned, which presumes that right knowledge is sufficient for good action and attributes evil to ignorance. Consequently, both de Lubac and Rahner lose the significance of the distinction between nature and the supernatural, and so subsume grace to creation. I have already noted the importance of Aquinas's understanding of the will, and here I will begin to retrieve his metaphysical insights that can help to resolve Augustine's dilemma.

Building on Augustine's differentiation of voluntary and natural activity, Aquinas states in *Summa theologiae* 1-2.10 that the will is the source of all voluntary and contingent activity: "[T]he will is distinguished from nature as one kind of cause from another; for some things happen naturally and some are done voluntarily."[84] Aquinas had previously argued in the *Prima pars* that the will was an "intellectual appetite." He thought of willing as an intellectual determination of desire that elicited desire, served as the power of that desire, and occasioned its free choice (1.80.1, 1.82.1).[85] The intellect judged an object to be worthy of being attained and, as the final cause of desire, moved the will to action (1.59.1; 1.80.1–2; 1.82.3–4; 1.83.2–4).[86]

Augustine had previously encountered the problems with this position, but it was Aquinas who recognized that it subjected the will to the necessity of the intellect's judgment. Any object the intellect judged to be good was simplistically assumed to be able to be willed. But the more important difficulty was the assumption that evil actions were caused by ignorance. Between writing *Prima pars* and *Prima secundae*, Aquinas recognized that this model was incoherent: it implied simultaneously that the will was necessarily moved by the intellect; and that it was (i.e., was Pelagian).[87] As Lottin showed, Aquinas reconceived the will as a spontaneous power of the soul that the intellect merely specified by supplying the formal rather than final cause of the will's activity.[88]

Considered in these terms, when the will accepts a good and acts to attain it, it is not the specific object that is sought, but the universal good communicated by that particular object. The will comes to share with that particular object in the good it communicates. This means that the will is first ordered to attain the universal good, which it seeks for the preservation of the general species, before it is ordered to the good of the individual (1.60.5.3 ad. and 1-2.109.3).[89] Willing the individual good first is disordered and will be frustrated, because it neither rightly knows nor wills the good. Therefore, happiness depends upon willing objects in the proper natural arrangment of their universal being (2-2.26).

Aquinas inherited this understanding of the order of charity (*ordo caritatis*) from Augustine.[90] As Aquinas interpreted it, the will naturally loves (*dilectio*), or seeks pleasure and delight in the world (1-2.26.3).[91] In doing so, it seeks both to attain the objects of its love (*amor concupiscentiae*) and to sustain loving relations (*amor amicitiae*) (1-2.26.4).[92] David Gallagher insists, in his reading of Aquinas, that this love is not egoistic for Aquinas, because desired objects (*concupiscence*) are always sought for the sake of a personal relation (friendship).[93] Aquinas, for example, quotes Aristotle, from *Rhetoric* 3.4: "[T]o love is to wish good to someone" (1-2.26.4). Friendship is the most universal context for the willing of individual objects of desire, and all love of objects must be cast in these terms if the desire for those objects is not to be sinful. Friendship is the most universal context for human willing, because all voluntary activity is carried out for a social reason, for the sake of a person (including oneself) or the relation between persons (1-2.26.4, 1-2.73.9).[94] Because the relation is the context and goal of the willing, the person is an end in herself and not an object or a means to another object (1.60.3).[95] The will is unique among the faculties in that it seeks to attain the universal good simply for its own sake, and the ultimate aim of all desired objects is to will the good relation of friendship with God, who is that Good.

The order of charity gives Aquinas a way to understand how a human act, through grace, cooperates with God's perfection of the universe (1-2.19.9–10). This is done where the intellectual apprehension of the abstract order of the cosmos is concretely willed as God's self-communication (2-2.26). This human cooperation with the divine operation in creation is itself an expression of the harmony of the created order, a perfection of the spiritual creature whose concrete existence realizes for itself the goodness of God communicated in creation (1.82.4; 1-2.8.1, 9.1–2, 10.2–4; 2-2.24.1).

However, although he sustains Augustine's order of charity, Aquinas understands created perfection differently than Augustine. Oliva Blanchette's study of the perfection of the universe in Aquinas makes clear the nature of his divergence from Augustine regarding the metaphysical nature of perfection.[96] For Augustine, God is absolute and immutable, because God is perfectly self-determined. But for Aquinas, perfection is not at all a proper predicate of God. Perfection implies that something that was previously coming-to-be (*fieri*) has now been moved to completion (*factum esse*) (1.4.4.1 ad.).[97] Augustine tended to think of God in exactly the terms in which Aquinas described the perfection of motion: "the attainment of the fullness of its nature and power according to its species."[98] God, for Augustine, is the full expression in the act of the nature and power of divinity for self-determination.[99] Whereas for Aquinas, God is simply the eternal activity of existing (*esse*). There is no essence of divinity that is perfectly expressed in the power of God's act. God's essence and act are the immediate identity of Being-itself (*ipsum esse*).

Accordingly, Aquinas has the metaphysical understanding of both the will and Being to sustain a mutual, noncompetitive social relation of friendship between God and humanity. The expression of the power of God's nature does not depend for him on a perfect act of self-determination. As the active operation of existing, God is neither a being among beings nor an agent among agents.[100] The multiplicity of beings and agents communicates the infinite being and goodness of God (1.60.5.3 ad.; 1.103; 1-2.19.4; 2-2.23.2).[101] Because multiplicity means greater complexity, it increases the probability for instability, entropy, and conflict for individuals. But greater multiplicity also increases the degree of infinite goodness that can be communicated by created being.[102] Increased differentiation thus increases the capacity for the perfection of the whole.[103] As Blanchette notes, the perfection of the universe is, for Aquinas, the harmonious order of the totality of created existence. That harmony is the implicit goal of all created motions.[104]

Despite these extraordinary developments toward understanding created existence as a social relation, Aquinas does not submit the immediate intuition of the hierarchical order of being, as enshrined in the order of charity, to critique. He does not question the authority of his actually existing social relations, but rather presumes they are natural expressions of the divine order of reality. Not only does this exclude any critical dimension from the exercise of charity, and thus reinforce the illusion of the "natural" order of his social relations, but it precludes the possibility of linking that critique to the theology of grace. The maxim "Grace perfects nature" will continue to be conceived not as a substantive transformation of the order of nature but as the reinforcing of the illusion that the existing social arrangement is coincident with the order of charity. Aquinas can recognize the perfection of nature must be a social relation of friendship with God, and he clearly knows that the equality demanded by friendship cannot be naturally willed by the human being.[105] Yet, when it is realized, this act of charity remains, insofar as it is conceived in these terms of immediate intuition, simply an extension and enlarging of the natural drive to self-preservation.

Aquinas admits this when he states that every object of the will is willed for oneself (1.60.3).[106] Even in beatitude, friendship with God and the perfection of charity express self-love (1.60.3). Beatitude unites this natural operation (concupiscence) immediately in harmony (*amicitiae*) with the universal, which includes oneself.[107] That union and perfection is ecstatic for the creature, because its own natural drive to self-preservation is in harmony with the whole cosmic order.[108] One's own good is willed at the level of the universal rather than the individual, which turns one outward in friendship to God, the neighbor, and the world rather than inward in self-seeking. Another's good is truly assumed as one's own, sought, attained, and enjoyed (*delectatio/gaudium*) (1-2.28.1–2).[109] And in this case, that other's good is God's, the universal good itself that perfects our drive to self-preservation. By willing God's good, we will the order of the whole cosmos and our place in it (1.23; 1.103; 1.116; 1-2.109; 1-2.112; 2-2.58). In this way, although he recognizes that the union of grace and creation is a social relation, Aquinas continues to subsume the critical concept of grace to the immediate intuition of the natural order and is incapable of recognizing the critique of his actually existing social relations that is implied in theology of grace.

Both Augustine and Aquinas recognized and sought to incorporate the will and social relations into their theologies of grace and metaphysics of creation. They both failed to attend to the intrinsically critical aspect of social relations and thus misidentified the social with the immediate experience of nature. As a result, the important vital distinctions Aquinas makes between will/intellect and natural/supernatural, which are the foundation for the metaphysical differentiation of grace from creation, cannot be sustained apart from a concurrent theology of grace as a critical social relation.

SIN AND GRACE: THE SOCIAL DIMENSION OF GRACE

It was Luther who recuperated this critical, social dimension of grace in his response to scholastic metaphysics. Central to that critique was his focus of Augustine's argument for the priority of grace as a social relation (rather than an infused habit), which was the basis for his insistence that charity and self-preservation are incompatible. Luther claimed that the scholastic concept of nature erroneously repeated a sinful social relation.[110] In doing so, Luther reverts from the advances made by Aquinas to the Augustinian–Lombardian notion that our acts of charity are not truly our own, but God's. Our love merely shares in God's charity. Ironically, Luther does not realize that the intellectualist idea of the will on which this understanding of charity was based specifically rejected by Aquinas in *Prima secundae* for being not only implicitly determinist but also Pelagian.

These aspects of Luther's theology have been well documented by the "new Finnish" interpretation of Luther, which has brought to light aspects of his doctrine of grace that have long been obscured.[111] Particularly significant to the Finns' argument is an emphasis on the important role ontology played in Luther's argument about justification, which they insist is entirely misunderstood when contrasted to metaphysics.[112] Tuomo Mannermaa has traced the roots of the antimetaphysical interpretation of Luther, which has become dominant, to Albrecht Ritschl's appropriation of Herman Lotze's neo-Kantianism. Ritschl made Lotze's distinction between logical validity and ethical value central to the meaning of the Reformation doctrine of justification in modern Protestant theology.[113] This had the effect of transforming the doctrine into a subjective apprehension of the ultimate value of existence, which the Finns argue changes the metaphysical assumptions of Luther's doctrine of justification. Luther, they insist, was a realist for whom knowledge of the form of Christ really united the knower to the divine nature.[114]

Despite sharing scholasticism's epistemology in this respect, Luther's different conclusions about justification were due to his different understanding of the form of faith. Where scholastic theology made charity the form of faith (*fides caritate formata*), Luther argued that Christ himself was that form of faith (*fides Christi formata*).[115] As a result, Luther understood justification to be the presence of Christ in the soul by faith, rather than the soul's own act of charitable cooperation with God (1-2.114.1).[116] Faith is our loving response of trust in Christ's prior love of us. In this sense, faith is not our own charitable knowledge of God through Christ but the expression in us of God's grace through Christ (1-2.62.4).[117] Our "proper" acts of love presuppose Christ's loving disposition and are expressions of our right relation to him.[118] On the basis of that love, the will is liberated to realize its true purpose by giving the self away rather than reinforcing its alienating pursuit of self-preservation.[119]

As significant a transformation of scholastic metaphysics as this is, Sammeli Juntunen nonetheless argues that it is incorrect to understand it as "antimetaphysical and antiontological."[120] The "personalist" paradigms that Gerhard Ebeling and Wilfried Joest use to interpret Luther are wrong to claim that all ontological questions are ipso facto "corrupted questions" for Luther (129). As Juntunen argues, it is right to describe Luther as "antimetaphysical" (in the sense of being more "relational and existential") not because of a "refusal of the concept of being" but because of "a certain understanding of love, which is fundamental for his theology" (131). Based on Luther's insistence that our charity is in fact God's charity, he also distinguishes between natural, self-preserving human love (*amor hominis*) and the intrinsically self-giving love of God (*amor dei*) (131–36). Juntunen summarizes Luther on God's love: "God is in his essence a pure, giving love whose motive is not to get good for himself, but to give good to that which lacks it in itself. God's love is creative; it never finds its object as something preexistent. Rather it turns to that which is nothing and is in itself needy in order to create it and make it existent and good through loving it" (131).

Juntunen says that Luther rejects human love as "egoistic," but it is more accurate, I believe, to understand Luther's objection as against the priority of the drive to self-preservation rather than self-bestowal (131). Not even human impulse to self-preservation is essentially evil for Luther. Rather, it is corrupt and incapable of charity by its own power (131). With these convictions, Luther submits the metaphysics of the order of charity (*ordo caritatis*) to critique. In its place, he develops a distinction between divine and human love that leads to a concurrent distinction between natural being (*esse naturae*) and graceful being (*esse gratiae*) (137). Both acknowledge the world as God's creation, a doctrine which Luther understands explicitly in the social terms of "being through an-other" (*ens per aliud*) (145–47). But the natural being, which gives rise to the human love of self-preservation, is ontologically transformed through union with Christ into graceful being, which is drawn into God's self-bestowal (147).

As Reijo Työrinoja notes, this indicates that in Luther's doctrine of justification Christ becomes the substantial form of the believer's soul, and by him the soul is drawn into the Trinitarian life of God.[121] These ontological consequences mean that Luther's justification is expressed explicitly in terms of deification (*theosis*).

On this particular point, it may be accurate to say that Luther shows greater metaphysical insight than Aquinas.[122] Luther's justification is an actualist doctrine, which repudiates the scholastic understanding of justification, in which merit is a product of a perfect human act of self-preservation, as metaphysically incoherent.[123] Aquinas had maintained, against the Augustinian–Lombardian thesis, that any truly charitable acts by a creature must be that creature's own. Yet Luther recognized that, if it is the case that the creature must produce its own act of charity, then charity could never be an actuality for the soul. If the infusion of the *habitus* of charity was merely an accidental rather than substantial transformation of the natural drive to self-preservation, charity would remain only an abstract ideal for human activity, an infinite and unrealized demand.[124] Anticipating Hegel's critique of Kant's categorical imperative, Luther saw that the scholastic conception of *habitus* actually implied the opposite of what it was taken to mean.[125] Where the concept of the *habitus* was intended to supply the basis by which the good (charity) could be performed, it actually resulted in its inversion in actual existence: namely, that charity can never actually be done *because* it is a reality that *ought to be* (but is not now) actual for the soul. The very idea of conceiving grace as infused *habitus* acknowledges this problem. The command for charity implies what ought to be a reality in the soul is not. This means that its good to which the soul is obliged is a good it cannot actually perform. If the soul was capable of that good, then it would do it.

Luther's critique maintains that the possibility of charity, which the infused *habitus* is meant to establish, can be for it only an abstract possibility. It is invoked for the sake of resolving the actual contradiction between a "natural" self-preservation and a "supernatural" charity. An infused, accidental *habitus* is meant to show that there is no logical inconsistency in the claim that the will should be charitable. Nonetheless, the obligation to do charity means that charity is not an actuality for it, that in fact must remain an actual impossibility. In these terms, charity can be only an abstract obligation with a negative relation to actually existing social reality.[126] These are the terms of the infinite practical obligation in which scholastic theology conceived of justification and which Luther criticized as the idolatrous repetition of self-preservation, and the sinful deformation of human nature.[127] The Finns' focus on the ontological dimension of Luther's doctrine, however, leads them to overlook the social significance of Luther's critique of self-preservation, which resists negative and abstract accounts of grace.[128]

Luther's critique of scholastic justification is surprisingly consistent with Aquinas's actualist metaphysics of God's Being. And on this basis, he vehemently rejects this model as an ironic denial of the reality and efficacy of God's grace. He links it directly to concupiscence, and calls it "robbery" of God.[129] Luther's doctrine of justification is affirming the metaphysical actuality of charity. As he states, the presence of the Holy Spirit alone must be enough for justification or, that presence is meaningless. "Meaningless" here should be understood to be as the reiteration of natural self-preservation, which is itself, under the conditions of sin, the expression of a broken relation with God. Justification by faith, in contrast, is the positive affirmation of the actuality of redemption, which is the prior presence and activity of God within us through our union with Christ. Thus, Luther's doctrine expands and elaborates on Aquinas's central metaphysical insights, but in a way that submits the immediate grasp of "nature" to conceptual critique by the cross and resurrection of Christ, and given new and fresh meaning. It is now in these terms the relation of nature to the cross and resurrection that is decisive, and the attempted definition of what is "natural" apart from the cross and resurrection is revealed to be a denial of God's grace, "robbery of God." It is for this reason that Luther insists on a real theological transformation of metaphysics rather than, as with the scholastic adoption of Aristotelian action theory, its uncritical adoption and deployment in theology.[130]

Nevertheless, the ontological dimension of Luther's thought, which the Finns rightly retrieve as situated at the heart of this doctrine, remains problematic. Though Luther has successfully recovered the concept of grace as a critical social relation, like Augustine before him, his christological inflection of ontological participation is unable to sustain a noncompetitive social relation between the divine and human wills. The encounter with Christ ontologically transforms the will's drive to self-preservation by drawing it into the self-giving Triune life of God, where, in union with Jesus Christ, Christ's action becomes the basis of our own, and thus the principle and goal of all good human action.[131] Luther's dependence on the Augustinian–Lombardian identification of charity with the Holy Spirit lacks the coherent account of the will that Aquinas established and reduces the social relation to an abstract subjective identity with the form of Christ. "Proper" acts of Christian subjects are merely predicates of the dominant subject, Jesus Christ. In this respect, deification for Luther will remain a "Christomonism."

CONCLUSION

In this chapter, I have isolated the two most important elements of the study thus far: Aquinas's metaphysics of the will and its attendant notion of the act of existence, and Luther's recuperation of the social and relational dimension of grace in his understanding of justification. My concern has been to show how Aquinas's metaphysics of the will is bound up with a notion of the act of existence that resolves the difficulties Augustine encountered in trying to overcome his implicitly competitive account of the God–world relation. In connection with this, the solution of these metaphysical difficulties comes at the price of a thoroughgoing reduction of the social and relational dimension of Augustine's mature theology of grace to the immediate intuition of nature.

It is on this specific point that Luther's doctrine of justification retrieved Augustine's insight into grace as a social relation and developed the critical standpoint that had remained undeveloped. When Luther rejects charity as the form of faith, it is for the metaphysically actualist reason that it transforms charity into an abstract and negative principle that has no significance for existing reality. Instead, he asserts that Christ himself must be the form of faith, through which one receives a right relation of actual union with God. It was in these terms that Luther recuperated the social and relational dimension of grace. Yet, just as he recuperated this dimension by referring it specifically to the person of Jesus, he conceives this formal element of Christ's saving work in overtly ontological terms that reduce the social relation between Jesus and the individual to one of identity. The Christian's submissive will becomes a predicate of Christ's, who dominates it, imposing (ironically) his own charitable one.

Despite this continued impasse in the attempt to unite grace and creation, we can now recognize the lineaments of a way forward. A coherent unity must depend on Aquinas's metaphysics of Being and the will, which yields a distinction of the will from the intellect and a noncompetitive relation between God and the creature. That account also demands a critical account of grace as a social relation, which retains the metaphysical actualism of the doctrines of justification and election in the Reformers. The union of the doctrines must confound any reduction of difference to identity, which specifically means their union must not be abstract or negative. The union of grace and creation must be historical and material. In sum, we must understand grace, explicitly, as an actually existing social relation. Chapter 5 offers a programmatic account of that union, drawn from the results of my study.

Notes

1. I take a tack different than Michael Hanby's suggestion that the divergences in Augustine's thought are best conceived according to the ontology in which they most properly cohere—that ontology being given, according to him, in *The Trinity*. Aside from the obvious point that *The Trinity* is itself not a coherent work, this is to overlook the importance for interpretation that Augustine's development represents. It is a mistake to presume to draw Augustine's thought into a coherent approach, as Hanby does, especially without attending to the problems he encountered in his genetic development. See Michael Hanby, *Augustine and Modernity*, Radical Orthodoxy (New York: Routledge, 2003). This also applies to the argument in Carol Harrison, *Rethinking Augustine's Early Theology: An Argument for Continuity* (New York: Oxford University Press, 2006).

2. See Gerhard May, *Creatio ex nihilo: The Doctrine of "Creation out of Nothing" in Early Christian Thought*, trans. A. S. Worrall (New York: T & T Clark, 2004), 62–84 and 179–80.

3. Ibid., 68, 71–73, and 179–80. The connection of this synthesis of the world-seed and a single divine act to the ontological account of the divine decree of election must be noted.

4. Ibid., 148–78.

5. Ibid., 74–76.

6. Indeed, Valentinian Gnosticism appears to have rejected two ultimate principles while having no particular concern to reject the logic of dualism. See ibid., 85–117.

7. See the discussion in Harrison, *Rethinking Augustine's Early Theology*, 74–114. Harrison uses the language of absolute dependence.

8. Carol Harrison argues, in ibid., that the dependence in Augustine's doctrine of creation can be the basis for an argument for continuity between Augustine's early and late theology. Her argument with J. P. Burns, however, which turns on rejecting the distinction between interior and exterior, does not account for the shift away from God's omnipresence in the early work, noted by Robert J. O'Connell in *Saint Augustine's Early Theory of Man, a.d. 386–391* (Cambridge, MA: Harvard University Press, 1968), to a focus on God's agency in bestowing grace, which is the focus of the later theology. She also notes that her argument for continuity between Augustine's early and later thought depends entirely on her ability to demonstrate continuity with regard to Augustine's teaching on the will (p. 203). Her argument, however, which consists in showing that Augustine never held to notion of the will that had no need of grace (235–36), significantly misses the point that Augustine's developing notion of the will specifically corresponds to his insight, against Origen, into the failure of a theology of grace based on persuasion to actually secure salvation. In this respect, the issues related to creation, grace, and the will that come into relief in Augustine's work are significantly more complex than Harrison's argument for continuity will allow us to recognize.

9. Manichaeanism understood the soul to be an originally divine element trapped now in an evil materiality. See Augustine, *Against Fortunatus* 19–22.

10. See O'Connell, *Saint Augustine's Early Theory of Man*; O'Connell, *The Origin of the Soul in St. Augustine's Later Works* (New York: Fordham University Press, 1987); and J. Patout Burns, "From Persuasion to Predestination: Augustine on Freedom in Rational Creatures," in *In Dominico eloquio = In Lordly Eloquence: Essays on Patristic Exegesis in Honor of Robert Louis Wilken*, ed. Paul M. Blowers et al. (Grand Rapids, MI: Eerdmans, 2002), 294–316.

11. Although I depart from his interpretation in many important ways, my discussion of the relationship between sovereignty, goodness, the will, and creation out of nothing owes much to the reading given in Rowan Williams, "Creation," in *Augustine through the Ages: An Encyclopedia*, ed. Allan D. Fitzgerald (Grand Rapids, MI: Eerdmans, 1999), 251–54.

12. See Augustine, *Against Fortunatus* 23–37.

13. This is most easily seen in ibid., 19–47.

14. See Williams, "Creation," 251–52. Williams first alerted me to the close interconnection of sovereignty, goodness, agency, and *creatio ex nihilo* in Augustine's thought. However, Williams

interprets Augustine's early discussion of "formlessness" during the anti-Manichaean period (particularly in *On Faith and the Creed* 2.2 [393 ce]) as anticipating the position of the *Literal Commentary on Genesis* by making a distinction between the one whose "mode of existence is one of potential *for* structured reality" and the one whose mode is the "realization of structures" (252). Williams then interprets the *creatio ex nihilo* of the early period in continuity with the *Literal Commentary* as "the setting in being of a living system destined to grow toward beauty and order, even if this beauty and order is not at any given moment fully apparent" (252). Williams notes a connection of this idea with Augustine's doctrine of predestination but nonetheless allows that "creation is completed simultaneously . . . and yet there is a real history of interaction between creator and creation" (252). Closer attention to the development of Augustine's theology of grace calls this interpretation into question. Whatever continuity there may be between the two accounts, it is markedly different after the Donast controversy (ca. 411 ce). As O'Connell has recognized, Augustine later realizes that absence of form and indeterminacy amount to the same. The pure positiality of form of Plotinian matter remains, in this respect, identical with the Manichaean idea. See O'Connell, *Origin of the Soul*; and *Saint Augustine's Early Theory of Man*.

15. See Augustine, *On the Catholic Way of Life and the Manichean Way of Life* 2.3, 5, 7; *Two Souls* 1–3; *Against Fortunatus* 23–47; *On the Nature of Good* 1.1–3, 6, 12, 18–19; and *Confessions* 5.20–21, 7.17–27.

16. See Augustine, *On the Nature of Good* 1.5–12; *Teaching Christianity*, ed. John E. Rotelle, trans. Edmund Hill, The Works of St. Augustine, pt. 1, vol. 11 (Hyde Park, NY: New City, 1996), 1.34–35; *On Genesis: A Refutation of the Manichees* 1.32; *Literal Commentary on Genesis* 8.31–32; *The Trinity*, ed. John E. Rotelle, trans. Edmund Hill, Works of St. Augustine, pt. 1, vol. 5 (Hyde Park, NY: New City, 1991), 8.5, 11.8; and *Confessions* 7.16–21.

17. Augustine, *Soliloquies* 1.2; *On the Catholic Way of Life* 2.4; *Two Souls* 8, 12; *Against Fortunatus* 18–21; *Confessions* 7.18–19; and *On Genesis* 2.43.

18. This persuasion is, for the early Augustine, the work of demons, who themselves sinned spontaneously. See Augustine, *On Free Choice* 3.10.31; and Burns, "From Persuasion to Predestination," 300–301. On the unintelligiblity of evil, see *On Free Choice* 2.41–46, 3.76; and *Trinity*, 8.5.

19. See the discussion of the will in Harrison, Rethinking Augustine's Early Theology, 198–237. Though I believe that Harrison is right to recognize the importance of the will for the early Augustine, she does not recognize any significant development in his notion of the will and does not see the development of his theology of grace as tracking with those insights into the will. Instead, continuity in the theology of grace is established through continuity in the nature of the will as the intellectual specification of desire. Yet, as I have argued, it is just the social location and determination of the will, rather than an its status as an intellectual appetite, that comes increasingly into view in Augustine's latest works in continuity with his mature theology of grace. Consequently, Harrison never recognizes that it is the important role of the will in the doctrine of creation that, once he recognizes the significance of the distinction between knowing and doing the good, will produce the incoherence between his theologies of creation and grace.

20. See Augustine, *Confessions* 7.1–7 and 21–27.

21. This discussion first appears in Augustine, *Teaching Christianity*, 1–2.5, ca. 396 ce; it is elaborated upon in *On Baptism* 1.8–9. See the discussion in Burns, *Development of Augustine's Doctrine*, 66–71. See also the discussions in J. Patout Burns, "The Eucharist as the Foundation of Christian Unity in North African Theology," *Augustinian Studies* 31, no. 1 (2001): 1–23; and J. Patout Burns, "Establishing Unity in Diversity," *Perspectives in Religious Studies* 32, no. 4 (2005): 381–99.

22. See Burns, "Eucharist as Foundation of Christian Unity."

23. See Augustine, *Trinity* 11.7, 15 and 14.5.

24. See Augustine, *Two Souls* 17. Quotation is taken from Augustine, *The Manichean Debate*, ed. Boniface Ramsey, trans. Roland Teske, The Works of Saint Augustine, part 1, vol. 19 (Hyde

Park, NY: New City, 2006). See James Wetzel, *Augustine and the Limits of Virtue* (New York: Cambridge University Press, 1992), 90.

25. In this regard, I follow Dihle, Kahn, Sorabji, and to an extent Wetzel. See Albrecht Dihle, *The Theory of Will in Classical Antiquity*, Sather Classical Lectures (Berkeley: University of California Press, 1982); Charles Kahn, "Discovering the Will: From Aristotle to Aquinas," in *The Question Of "Eclecticism": Studies in Later Greek Philosophy*, ed. John M. Dillon and A. A. Long (Berkeley: University of California Press, 1988), 234–59; and Richard Sorabji, "The Concept of the Will from Plato to Maximus the Confessor," in *The Will in Human Action: From Antiquity to the Present Day*, ed. Thomas Pink and M. W. F. Stone (New York: Routledge, 2004). The language of "invention" is from Wetzel, *Augustine and the Limits of Virtue*, 3. Wetzel is a unique voice in the discussion represented by Dihle, Kahn, and Sorabji. He has a nuanced account of this difference, arguing that the will is still, for Augustine, essentially a matter of desire. See Wetzel, 7–10. However, Wetzel recognizes and notes the importance for Augustine of the distinction between the good that we know and our inability to do it. See *Augustine and the Limits of Virtue*, 86–87.

26. Wetzel, *Augustine and the Limits of Virtue*, 90. I should note here as well the difference of the claims I am making about Augustine's insight into the distinction of the will from the intellect and desire, and Aquinas as the first unambiguous articulation of the will in distinction from the intellect and desire. I understand Augustine to be the first to begin to articulate a unique notion of the will, but the status of this notion remained vague and incoherently expressed to the end of his work and through his legacy in the medieval period. It is with Aquinas, and specifically in the *Prima secundae* (I maintain with Lottin and Lonergan) that we have the first coherent articulation of Augustine's idea.

27. See Sorabji, "Concept of the Will," 6–28.

28. This is one of the moments when Augustine appears at his closest to Stoicism and its idea of the justice of natural law. With this notion of personal volition, however, Augustine departs significantly from Stoicism.

29. Robert Crouse, "*Paucis mutatis verbis*: Saint Augustine's Platonism," in *Augustine and His Critics*, ed. Robert Dodaro and George Lawless (New York: Routledge, 2000), 37–50.

30. My discussion of the will in Plotinus, and his influence on Augustine, is indebted to Vernon J. Bourke, *Will in Western Thought: An Historico- Critical Survey* (New York: Sheed & Ward, 1964), 80–81 and 193–97.

31. See ibid., 193.

32. Plotinus, *Ennead* 6.8.21. The quotation, including the Greek, is taken from ibid., 195.

33. For a discussion of emanation and necessity in Plotinus, see John M. Rist, *Plotinus: The Road to Reality* (Cambridge: Cambridge University Press, 1977), 66–83. Rist argues that *necessity* is not the appropriate word to describe the emanations from the One, because the One wills to be as the One is. Such a response would clearly not suffice for sovereignty as it is here being construed (see also *Ennead* 4.8.21). Furthermore, although there is a role for providence in the Plotinian system, that role is fulfilled by Nous, not by the Ultimate itself (see *Ennead* 3.2–3; and Rist, 89). Finally, as I will make clear, it is the very self-determination of this willing that leads it ineluctably to an affirmation of necessity. On the significance of omnipresence for the Neoplatonic conception of the Good, see O'Connell, *Origin of the Soul*, 45–51.

34. Plotinus, *Ennead* 6.8.21. The quotation, including the Greek, is taken from Bourke, *Will in Western Thought*, 195. The reader should note the coincidence between this account and the negative determination at work in Descartes, Spinoza, and Hegel. There is a sense here in which Plotinus is the necessary precursor to Hegel insofar as each understands the development of the world to be a necessary consequence of the Absolute's reflexive self-knowledge and constitution. Augustine, by contrast, insists that the world arises as the result of the gratuitous act of an agency.

35. Augustine, *Catholic Way of Life*, quoted in Harrison, *Rethinking Augustine's Early Theology*, 90–91 (emphasis original). Harrison cites this passage to illustrate Augustine's appreciation for God as Being. For further demonstration of this point, see Augustine, *Confessions*

8.1 and *Teaching Christianity* 1.8.8. See also Richard Sorabji, *Time, Creation, and the Continuum: Theories in Antiquity and the Early Middle Ages* (Chicago: University of Chicago Press, 2006), 239. This recognition that the "contrary of existence is non-existence" is what Étienne Gilson specified as the realization of the ontological difference in Augustine, which sets him on a path distinct from Plotinus. See Gilson, *The Christian Philosophy of Saint Augustine*, Random House Lifetime Library (New York: Random House, 1960).

36. Augustine, *Catholic Way of Life*, quoted in Harrison, *Rethinking Augustine's Early Theology*, 90–91. This would clearly be an example of Heideggerian "ontotheology" and an example of the "metaphysics of the will."

37. See *On Free Choice* 1.8–15. See also *Confessions* 10 (esp. 18), and 11.20, 26, 27; 12.9, 12, 23.

38. See *Confessions* 10.18–19.

39. See ibid., 7.16–24 and bk. 10.

40. See Plato, *Phaedrus* 245–46c, where the soul is designated as self-moving, perpetually in motion, and therefore immortal.

41. Augustine, *Two Souls*, 14; quotation is taken from *Manichean Debate*. See *On Free Choice* 1.8–15; and Sorabji, "Concept of the Will," 9.

42. Risto Saarinen, *Weakness of the Will in Medieval Thought: From Augustine to Buridan*, Studien und Texte zur Geistesgeschichte des Mittelalters (Leiden, Neth.: Brill, 1994), 22. Throughout this chapter, I refer to this concept of the will as self-determination as "Platonic." I intend by this only the suggestion that this idea begins with Plato's notion of the soul as that which "moves itself." I acknowledge that Augustine's use of the term owes much to Stoic ideas, which were largely mediated through Neoplatonism. For a discussion of this connection, see Wetzel, *Augustine and the Limits of Virtue*, 10–12 and 68–76.

43. Risto Saarinen, *Weakness of the Will in Medieval Thought: From Augustine to Buridan*, Studien und Texte zur Geistesgeschichte des Mittelalters (Leiden, Neth.: Brill, 1994), 22.

44. See J. Patout Burns, "Grace: The Augustinian Foundations," in *Christian Spirituality, Origins to the Twelfth Century*, ed. Bernard McGinn and John Meyendorff (New York: Crossroad, 1985), 331–49; and Burns, "From Persuasion to Predestination," 294–316. Augustine's early dependence on Platonic presumption of the intellect's determination of choice is made in different and complimentary ways by these two essays.

45. This recognition initially appeared to Augustine in the form of a conflict within the self between what is desired and the capacity to achieve the desired object. Yet, as James Wetzel argues, the context for Augustine's discussion is a treatment of habit. Wetzel suggests that the self fails to will the newly recognized good not because of a deficiency in the willing but because of its having been habitually shaped according to a different good. This is not so much a conflict within the self as a differentiation between the perception and execution of competing goods. See Wetzel, *Augustine and the Limits of Virtue*. This marks recognition of the difference between the intellectual apprehension of the good and its performance by the will, which takes Augustine beyond Stoicism in that it involves not merely the differentiation of willing from desire but the further distinction of the will from the intellect, which sets the stage for Aquinas's development.

46. Note the discussion of the good and the will in *The Trinity*, ed. John E. Rotelle, trans. Edmund Hill, *Works of St. Augustine*, 8.5. There, Augustine notes that "the good the soul turns to in order to be good is the good from which it gets its being. This is when the will accords with nature to perfect the soul in good, when the will turns in love toward that good by which the soul is what it does not forfeit being, even if the will turns away again. . . . So the will can forfeit what the will can obtain; the soul was already there to will to turn toward that from which it was, but it was not already there to will to be before it was." That he moves, directly after this statement, to a discussion of the relationship of this love to the truth, in 8.6–8, is significant. It points to his difficulty in separating the respective objects of intellect and will. As he says in 8.10, true love is simply "cleaving to the truth," but this truth itself is defined as to "love [one's] brother, and to love that love," which simply is God (8.12–14). This point should be viewed as well in combination

with 9.12, in which Augustine insists that nothing is properly willed that is not, "previously uttered as a word in his heart," as an "interior word." He further associates the will with that which directs the mind's attention in 10.12 (and 11.7), and then further asserts, in 10.13, that the will is present for us to "use" or "enjoy" things. In this regard, it points to the mind's particular use and enjoyment of itself and is meant to be a way of redirecting the mind away from "sensible" things and toward the apprehension of truth within itself (10.11, 11.7). The will is further noted as a certain "repose" in things that are "delighted in for their own sakes" (10.13). It is in each of these elements that Augustine has recognized but not yet understood how it is that the will as distinct from the intellect is ordered toward the good in connection with the true. The increased moral and ethical orientation to the will is also clearly recognizable in 11.7–8. All "wishes are straight, and all the ones linked with them too, if the one to which they are all referred is good; but if that is bent then they are all bent. And thus a sequence of straight wishes or wills is a ladder for those who would climb to happiness, to be negotiated by definite steps; but a skein of bent and twisted wishes or wills is a rope to bind anyone who acts so" (11.10).

47. Burns, "From Persuasion to Predestination," 304–6.

48. Augustine, *Retractions* 1.15.4. Quotation is taken from *Manichean Debate*. Augustine's earlier writings emphasize the metaphysical significance of order, whereas his later writings rely heavily on justice, which was a classically political, civic, and ethical virtue. The priority of justice is displayed most prominently in his writings against Julian, particularly the *Unfinished Answer to Julian* 1.37: "If God is the origin of justice, as you [Julian] say, why do you not admit that justice is given to human beings by God? Why do you want justice to be the choice of the human will rather than the gift of God?" Quotation from Augustine, *Answer to the Pelagians to the Monks of Hadrumetum and Provence*, ed. John E. Rotelle, trans. Roland Teske, The Works of St. Augustine, pt. 1, vol. 26 (Hyde Park, NY: New City,1999). See also 1.45–47, 79–80, 127, 133.

49. The discussion of the interconnectedness of goodness, use, enjoyment, love of God, and love of neighbor appears in Augustine, *Teaching Christianity*, ed. John E. Rotelle, trans. Edmund Hill, The Works of St. Augustine, 1.3–9, 20–44.

50. The clearest case of this is perhaps Augustine's discussion of the pride that preceded the performance of the first sin in the lately composed *City of God* 14.11–14. Particularly important is this statement: "The choice of the will, then, is genuinely free only when it is not subservient to faults and sins. God gave it that true freedom, and now that it has been lost, through its own fault, it can be restored only by him who had the power to give it at the beginning" (14.11). All quotations of this text are taken from Augustine, *City of God*, trans. Henry Scowcroft Bettenson (New York: Penguin, 1984).

51. Thus goodness is marked as coincident with the constitution of otherness. Though I believe this is a necessary corollary of Augustine's position, it is explicitly anticipated in his work at a number of places, most notably the paradoxical discussion of enjoyment, use, and goodness in *Teaching Christianity* 1.31–34. Augustine notes here that God's "making use of us is directed to his goodness," which is manifested in our existence; and this "use, therefore, by which God is said to make use of us is directed to our benefit and not to his, but only to his goodness." This associates the goodness of the act of creating with the enjoyment of the "otherness" of the creature in its "otherness," decisively not for the purpose of accomplishing anything or attaining anything for God. This marks a sharp break with reflective self-determination. The same point is at work in Augustine's exhortations to charity in the Donatist controversy. See, for example, *On Baptism*, 1.8–9 and 17–19.

52. See *City of God*, 14.12: "But God's instructions demanded obedience, and obedience is in a way the mother and guardian of all the other virtues in a rational creature, seeing that the rational creation has been so made that it is to man's advantage to be in subjection to God, and it is calamitous for him to act according to his own will, and not obey the will of his Creator."

53. See the point made by Wetzel, *Augustine and the Limits of Virtue*, 17–26.

54. For a discussion of this connection, see John Rist, "Augustine on Free Will and Predestination," *Journal of Theological Studies* 20, no. 2 (1969): 420–42. See also the response by D.

J. MacQueen, "Augustine on Free Will and Predestination: A Response to John Rist," *Museum Africum* 3 (1974).

55. My discussion of Augustine's spiritualism (illuminationism), his understanding of salvation history, and the development of his theology of grace is indebted to J. Patout Burns, "Grace: The Augustinian Foundation," in *Christian Spirituality: Origins to the Twelfth Century*, ed. Bernard McGinn, John Meyendorff, and Jean Leclerq (New York: Crossroad, 2000), 331–49.

56. The connection to de Lubac and the version of Augustinianism he advocated should be clear. This is also the kind of vision developed by Rahner.

57. See Burns, "Grace: The Augustinian Foundations," 331–49. Burns notes that Augustine incorporates this illuminationism into his account of salvation history. God's calling of Israel begins the process by which God educates humanity about individual and social sin. Giving the Law and sending the prophets restores the knowledge of the good that was lost in the fall, establishing a people committed to the good (To Simplician 1.1.1–6). For a later elaboration on its implications, see also Burns, "From Persuasion to Predestination," 294–316.

58. My discussion of this development is dependent especially on Burns, *Development of Augustine's Doctrine*, see especially 39–44; "Grace," 331–49; and "From Persuasion to Predestination," 294–316. See *To Simplician* 1.1 and 1.2. As Burns has argued, of particular importance was Romans 9:16: "It is not a matter of willing or of running, therefore, but of a merciful God" (see 1.2.10.) See Burns, 39–44.

59. Burns, "Grace," 331–49.

60. *To Simplician* 1.1.4, 1.2.16–17, 1.2.19–20.

61. Ibid., 1.1.2, 7.

62. *Confessions* 8.20–29.

63. *To Simplician* 1.1.7–11, 1.2.16–19.

64. Despite Wetzel's brilliant rereading of the Augustinian will as coextensive with desire, he fails to recognize the fundamental point that the issue at stake is not only that of a virtuous correspondence or the habitual vice that prevents its attainment as an objective good; Augustine is also investigating what it means to will the good for itself alone, which, though involving desire, intellect, and virtue, is pointing toward a unique operation.

65. *To Simplician* 1.1.17, 1.2.21, 2.1.8, 10–11.

66. Ibid., 1.2.

67. Burns, "From Persuasion to Predestination," 306.

68. Ibid., 307–9; see also Burns, *Development of Augustine's Doctrine*, 53–88.

69. See the discussion in J. Patout Burns, *Cyprian the Bishop*, Routledge Early Church Monographs (New York: Routledge, 2002), 166–76.

70. See Augustine, *Unfinished Work in Answer to Julian* 1.37, 1.45–47, 1.127, 1.133, 3.114, 5.38.5–6; *Answer to Julian* 1.45, 4.30; and *The Grace of Christ* 1.10.

71. Burns argues that this conflict arises first in the Donatist controversy as a concession to the necessity for coercion (*Development of Augustine's Doctrine*, 53–88).

72. Augustine, *The Gift of Perseverance* 20.52 and 21.55. See also ibid., 124–40.

73. Burns, "From Persuasion to Predestination," 309.

74. Burns, "From Persuasion to Predestination," 309–14.

75. Robert J. O'Connell, *The Origin of the Soul in Augustine's Later Works* (New York: Fordham University Press, 1987).

76. See Burns, *Development of Augustine's Doctrine*, 53–88.

77. See Augustine, *City of God* 5.8–11, bks. 11–12, 14.26–28. This is the reason Augustine insisted throughout his writings that the Neoplatonists possessed everything they needed except the incarnation, but this meant they mediated only death (see *Confessions* 7.27).

78. See *City of God* 5.8–11, where Augustine includes free acts of the will within the natural order of causes, "which is," he says, "for God, fixed, and is contained in his foreknowledge, since human acts of will are the causes of human activities. Therefore he who had prescience of the

causes of all events certainly could not be ignorant of our decisions, which he foreknows as the causes of our actions." He then goes on to associate this directly with a form of necessity, in chapter 10, where "we define 'necessity' in the sense implied when we say that it is necessary a thing should be thus, or should happen thus," concluding that he sees "no reason to fear that this would rob us of free will." This discussion of necessity should be read in combination with the discussion of creation of angels and human beings in 22.1–2.

79. See, for example, ibid., 11.33–12.5. The culprit here is Augustine's understanding of willing in the exercise of that sovereignty. Augustine insists that this does not render God the efficient cause of evil, but a positive role of this negation is affirmed. A theory of reprobation seems, thus, ineluctable. See Burns, *Development of Augustine's Doctrine*, 175–78.

80. See Augustine, *Confessions* 7.17; and *Trinity* 7.12. The order and goodness of the Origin that is reflected in creation applies only to the whole and is only relatively perceptible from the perspective of a given part of the whole. This relativity is essential to Augustine's account of creation and is intimately tied to his understanding of finitude's direct association with temporality. On the dynamic, temporal qualities of creation, see Williams, "Creation," 251–54. Augustine's appropriation of the category of Form allowed him to conceive the goodness of the created order on the analogy of a piece of music, wherein the composite of different finite potencies and acts express creation as it exists eternally in the Divine Mind in much the same way that the collective notes come together as the symphony envisioned by its composer. On this point, see Robert J. O'Connell, *Art and the Christian Intelligence in St. Augustine* (Cambridge, MA: Harvard University Press, 1978), 50–90.

81. See Augustine, *Literal Commentary on Genesis* 6.10.17 and 6.11.18–19. See also Williams, "Creation," 252.

82. Although the idea is Stoic in origin, Augustine most likely received the notion from Plotinus. See Plotinus, *Enneads* 2.1 and 3.1.7.

83. See May, *Creatio ex nihilo*, 70–73. See Augustine, *Literal Commentary on Genesis* 5.23.45 (see also Williams, "Creation," 252.)

84. See Thomas Aquinas, *ST* 1–2.10.1.1 ad. (Hereafter, this source will be cited in the text.) This discussion on the mechanics of the will, as well as the Latin, in Aquinas is throughout dependent on the analyses in David M. Gallagher, "The Will and Its Acts (Ia Iiae, Qq. 6–17)," in *The Ethics of Aquinas*, ed. Stephen J. Pope (Washington, DC: Georgetown University Press, 2002); Eberhard Schockenhoff, "The Theological Virtue of Charity (Iia Iiae, Qq. 23–46)," in Pope, *Ethics of Aquinas*; Daniel Westberg, *Right Practical Reason: Aristotle, Action, and Prudence in Aquinas* (New York: Oxford University Press, 1994); and Westberg, "Good and Evil in Human Acts (Ia Iiae, Qq 18–21)," in Pope, *Ethics of Aquinas*.

85. This understanding of appetite as desire and the power by which desire arises is from Gallagher, "Will and Its Acts," 86n5. See also *ST* 1.83.3–4. *ST* 1.83.2 is of special concern for noting that free will is to be understood specifically as a "power" and not simply as a habit or power and habit together. *ST* 1.83.3 further specificies that this power is "appetitive."

86. Denys Turner, *Thomas Aquinas: A Portrait* (New Haven: Yale University Press, 2013), 174–81.

87. See Mary Jo Lozzio, Self-Determination and the Moral Act: A Study of the Contribution of Odon Lottin, O.S.B. (Louvain, Belg.: Peeters, 1995),11–51; and Bernard Lonergan, Grace and Freedom, 193–99.

88. Odon Lottin, La theorie du libre arbitre depuis S. Anselme jusqu'a S. Thomas d'Aquin (Louvain: St. Maximin, 1929); Psychologie et Morale aux XIIe et XIIIe siècles. 6 volumes (Gembloux: Duculot, 1943–54), 1:221–62, 345–46, 374–75, 382–87 and 3:590–91; and see"La preuve de la liberté humaine chez Thomas d'Aquin," Recherches de théologie ancienne et médiévale 23 (1956): 325. The same argument was made and defended by Otto Pesch, "Philosophie und Theologie der Freiheit bei Thomas Aquin in quaest. Disp. 6 De malo" (Münchener Theologische Zeitschrift 13 (1962): 1–25; George Klubertanz, "The Root of Freedom in St. Thomas's Later Works" Gregorianum 42 (1961): 701–24; and Klaus Riesenhuber, "The

Bases and Meaning of Freedom in Thomas Aquinas," in American Catholic Philosophical Association 48 (1974): 99–111; and Die Tranzendenz der Freiheit zum Gutten: Der Wille in der Anthropologie und Metaphysik des Thomas von Aquin (Munich: Berchmanskolleg Verlag, 1971).

89. See Gallagher, "Will and Its Acts," 72.

90. This should be supplemented with the discussion at 1.60.5.3 ad. and 1-2.109.3. My discussion of the significance of the *ordo caritatis* in this chapter is indebted to Sammeli Juntunen, "Luther and Metaphysics: What Is the Structure of Being according to Luther?," in *Union with Christ: The New Finnish Interpretation of Luther*, ed. Carl E. Braaten and Robert W. Jenson (Grand Rapids, MI: Eerdmans, 1998), 129–60. The reader should also consult Juntunen, *Der Begriff des Nichts bei Luther in den Jahren von 1510 bis 1523*, Schriften der Luther-Agricola-Gesellschaft A36 (Helsinki, Fin.: Luther-Agricola-Gesellschaft, 1996). The most comprehensive analysis and history of the concept is given in Antti Raunio, *Summe des christlichen Lebens: Die "Goldene Regel" als Gesetz ser Liebe in der Theologie Martin Luthers von 1510–1527* (Mainz, Ger.: Von Zabern, 2001), 56–124.

91. Not *delectatio*, which is the enjoyment of a good attained. See Gallagher, "Will and Its Acts," 84.

92. See ibid; see also *ST* 1.60.3.

93. Gallagher, "Will and Its Acts," 84–85.

94. Gallagher (ibid., 84n43) notes that Aquinas understands love of friendship to include love of concupiscence, citing *De div. nom.*, chapter 4, lect. 9, n. 405.

95. Gallagher notes an important connection with Kant here. See ibid., 85.

96. Oliva Blanchette, "The Logic of Perfection in Aquinas," in *Thomas Aquinas and His Legacy*, ed. David M. Gallagher, Studies in Philosophy and the History of Philosophy (Washington, DC: Catholic University of America Press, 1994), 107–30. This article in many ways represents the argument of Blanchette's larger study, *The Perfection of the Universe*. Referring to the *Oxford English Dictionary*, he notes that there are three dominant English definitions of *perfection*. The first is "to be fully accomplished, thoroughly versed and skilled in some activity." The second, which is the one most commonly associated at present with God, is "the state of complete excellence, free from any flaw or imperfect quality." As I discussed in the previous chapter, Augustine's understanding of the divine simplicity is a combination of the two, namely, a fully accomplished self-determinate excellence. Yet there is a third definition, which became obsolete in English before the last century. This definition implies the idea of something that is "thoroughly made, formed, done, performed, carried out, accomplished." This was the definition implied by Aquinas's word *perfectum*, to which no reference to divinity was included. I have relied on Blanchette's analysis throughout the present discussion.

97. As Blanchette notes, the word *perfection* is formed from the Latin *facere* or *fieri*, meaning "to be made" or "to become." See Blanchette, "Logic of Perfection in Aquinas," 107–16.

98. Ibid., 110.

99. See the helpful discussion of Lonergan on *actus perfecti* and *imperfecti* in J. Michael Stebbins, *The Divine Initiative: Grace, World-Order, and Human Freedom in the Early Writings of Bernard Lonergan* (Toronto: University of Toronto Press, 1995). The form is therefore understood as the *actus imperfecti* of the thing, which is actualized in and through the act of the thing that is more properly understood as the *actus perfecti*. This distinction is also noted in Blanchette, *Perfection of the Universe*. See also Blanchette, ibid., 107–16.

100. This is the basic Heideggerian misunderstanding as regards the category of ontotheology.

101. The reader is directed to the discussion of the perfection of the universe at Blanchette, "Logic of Perfection in Aquinas," 116–25. The idea is that a whole composed of differentiated parts, working in harmony, is a greater manifestation of the good than an undifferentiated whole.

102. Blanchette uses the example of a lake to illustrate the point: a body of water exhibits a greater degree of continuity and stability than does an animal, but that stability comes at the cost of a decreased differentiation. See ibid., 107–130.

103. See ibid., 118.

104. See ibid., 116.

105. Gallagher, "Will and Its Acts," 84–85.

106. See ibid., 84.

107. Aquinas explicitly notes that every act aims at the universal good and not simply at the fulfillment of itself. But what is in question here is the sense in which the universal good is willed directly, for its own sake, as the expression of one's friendship with God and not for oneself (in the sense of including oneself in the universal). See *ST* 1.60.5; 1-2.28.2–3; 1-2.109. 3.1; 2-2.180.1. On this point, see Gallagher, ibid., 72.

108. This good is not impersonal, nor is it directed at the cosmos as such. On the contrary, the good of the universe as a whole, including as it does the totality of all persons, is itself only a good among goods, not the Good per se. Moreover, the ecstatic good that is actualized here is personal, because it is the universal Good that is Godself, whose greater comprehensiveness includes oneself, one's neighbor, and God. See *ST* 1-2.28.3 and 2-2.180.1.

109. See Gallagher, "Will and Its Acts," 85.

110. See Simo Peura, "Christ as Favor and as Gift (*Donum*): The Challenge of Luther's Understanding of Justification," in Braaten and Jenson, *Union with Christ*, 48–49. Peura notes that Luther's commentary on Lombard's *Sentences* shows that he associated this gesture with the immediate presence of the Holy Spirit, operating to produce good works. Aquinas himself specifically rejects this view, which is associated with just the social and relational dimension of grace found in Augustine. See *ST* 1.23.2.

111. Though much of my own reading of Luther stands in marked contrast to aspects of the Finns' interpretation of the consequences of their work, I find their basic thesis convincing.

112. This element is emphasized throughout the Finns' work. See especially Raunio, *Summe des christlichen Lebens*, 53–56 and 319–62.

113. See Tuomo Mannermaa, "Why is Luther So Fascinating? Modern Finnish Luther Research" in *Union with Christ: The New Finnish Interpretation of Luther*, eds. Carl E. Braaten and Robert W. Jenson (Grand Rapids: Eerdmans), 4–9.

114. See Tuomo Mannermaa, *Christ Present in Faith: Luther's View of Justification*, ed. Kirsi Irmeli Stjerna (Minneapolis: Fortress Press, 2005), 23–30. The German is *Der im Glauben gegenwärtige Christus: Rechtfertigung und Vergottung zum ökumenischen Dialog*, Arbeiten zur Geschichte und Theologie des Luthertums 8 (Hannover, Ger.: Lutherisches, 1989), 30–40.

115. See Reijo Työrinoja, "*Opus Theologicum*: Luther and Medieval Theories of Action," *Neue Zeitschrift für Systematische Theologie und Religionsphilosophie* 44, no. 2 (2002): 119–53.

116. Compare Luther's position here with Aquinas on merit at ST 1-2.114.1.

117. Compare Luther's position here to Aquinas on the order of the theological virtues at ST 1-2.62.4.

118. See Peura, "Christ as Favor and as Gift," 53–56.

119. See ibid., 134n22.

120. Juntunen, "Luther and Metaphysics," 129. Subsequent references to this source are cited in the text.

121. See Työrinoja, "*Opus Theologicum*."

122. As an example of what I have in mind with this point, which may seem somewhat sensational, if not provocative, is the distinction between goodness and rightness that is made in James Keenan, S.J., *Goodness and Rightness in Thomas Aquinas'* Summa Theologiae. Though Luther does not appear in Keenan's argument, one can easily recognize, especially from Keenan's analysis of charity, that Luther's argument for "alien" and "proper" righteousness depends on that very distinction. Perhaps it would be more accurate to say Luther has greater "theological" rather than "metaphysical" acuity, as the point is doctrinal for Luther and not speculative at all (in keeping

with the basic paradigmatic differences between the two). Nonetheless, I am suggesting that this doctrinal point is a more consistent expression of this metaphysical insight. Indeed, when reading *ST* 1-2.113, it appears as though Aquinas is struggling to map the existing high medieval Roman understanding of the economy of merit and ecclesial mediation onto this point, as he clearly thinks of justification as the product or effect or perfection of a motion of the will (infused grace, movement of freewill toward God in faith, movement of free will away from sin, and remission of sins [*ST* 1-2.113.6]). Despite the Lutheran World Federation and the Roman Catholic Church's *Joint Declaration on the Doctrine of Justification* (Grand Rapids, MI: Eerdmans, 2000), this is not compatible with Luther's point, nor is it accurate to say that this is a different language for expressing that same point. Quite the contrary, insofar as justification is thought of at all as the perfection of a motion, it is a flawed interpretation from Luther's perspective. The key to recognizing this is what is at stake in his rejection of the speculative paradigm.

123. Työrinoja, "*Opus Theologicum,*" says it is medieval action theory in general that is rejected as illusion. See also Theodor Dieter, *Der junge Luther und Aristoteles: Eine historisch-systematische Untersuchung zum Verhältnis von Theologie und Philosophie* (Berlin: de Gruyter, 2001).

124. At this point and in just this way, Aquinas's metaphysics takes on an idealistic rather than a realist cast.

125. On this point, see the exposition in Rose, *Hegel Contra Sociology*, 201–5.

126. This is what Hooker claimed in his early work on justification, noting that "double justification" was required in the Roman Catholic perspective, such that the term was effectively meaningless. See Corneliu C. Simut, *Richard Hooker and His Early Doctrine of Justification: A Study of His Discourse of Justification* (Burlington, VT: Ashgate, 2005), 55–58.

127. Lutheran theologians have continued to insist, even in the wake of the *Joint Declaration*, that concupiscence is not an appropriate category for discussing justification. See Veli-Matti Kärkkäinen, *One with God: Salvation as Deification and Justification*, Unitas Books (Collegeville, MN: Liturgical, 2004), 105–8.

128. See Anja Ghiselli, Kari Kopperi, and Rainer Vinke, eds., *Luther und Ontologie: Das Sein Christi im Glauben als strukturierendes Prinzip der Theologie Luthers: Referate der Factagung des Instituts für Systematische Theologie der Universität Helsinki in Zusammenarbeit mit der Luther-Akademie Ratzeburg in Helsinki 1.-5.4.1992*, Veröffentlichungen der Luther-Akademie Ratzeburg 21 (Helsinki, Fin.: Luther-Agricola-Gesellschaft,1993).

129. See Paul Althaus, *The Theology of Martin Luther* (Philadelphia: Fortress Press, 1966), 144–52.

130. See Työrinoja, "*Opus Theologicum.*"

131. See Mannermaa, *Christ Present in Faith*, 13–30.

5

A Reconstruction

The Union of Creation and Grace as a Social Relation

In the first chapter, I argued that the modern split between the subject and nature, founded on bourgeois selfhood, posed a number of problems for modern theology to which the articulation of the unity of grace and creation has been seen as the remedy. I argued that, because the experience of the division is determined by bourgeois social relations, any proposed solution will only repeat the problem. Whether the reunion is thought in terms of intuitive immediacy or conceptual mediation, it will remain abstract and negative.

Contemporary Catholic theology has sought that unity in a metaphysics of the immediate intuition of grace in creation. The concept of the supernatural developed in medieval theology specifically in order to distinguish the gratuity of creation from the gratuity of grace. It is this distinction that de Lubac and Rahner do not sustain in their common appeals to the preconceptual experience of grace. As a result, their rightful recuperation of the natural desire for the supernatural results in a concept of grace that is subsumed into creation. This is most apparent in their reliance on an intellectual illuminationism in which knowledge of the good is presumed to correlate immediately with the capacity for its performance, a concept of the will as an "intellectual appetite" that Aquinas rejected as both determinist and Pelagian. They thus have no sense in which to talk about the supernatural in terms of the will's innate inability to produce an act of charity. The immediate union of grace with creation forestalls any critical concept of grace that would allow the social determination of this assumption to be recognized as specifically bourgeois. Apart from a critical concept of grace as a social relation, the unity of grace and creation they articulate remains abstract and negative, unwittingly perpetuating the division and reinforcing our actually existing social fragmentation.

The same result occurs from the Protestant unions. Abjuring metaphysics, Protestant theology favors the critical principle of grace as a social relation, which resists its immediate conflation with creation. Grace is the experience of God's interruption of the drive to self-preservation amid the division from nature, and the imposition of redemption, which reveals the truth about reality and reconciles the self within its experience of alienation. Schleiermacher and Barth both develop the doctrine of election as the ontological category of the eternal divine decree in which God's grace is united with creation. On this model, grace cannot be subsumed into creation, and its status as a social relation is affirmed.

Nevertheless, the inverse is true. Creation is dominated by God's imposition of grace. Because the self's immediate experience is of a spontaneous separation from nature, as with de Lubac and Rahner, its capacity for self-determination remains inviolable. With the right concept of reality as eternally ordered to fellowship with God, the subject can reconcile the divided aspects of experience. Yet this model, too, is abstract and negative. It elevates the separation of grace from creation to a transcendental status in the divine decree, and unifies only in the concept. Again, this model reinforces the social divisions that give rise to the experience of alienation.

Both the Catholic metaphysical immediacy of grace and the Protestant status of grace as a social relation derive from the writings of Augustine. His early theology of creation, framed against Manichaean theology, argued that God's immutability ensures the goodness of material creation. Evil is a moral condition of the will, not an ontological reality. Evil is the illusion of the spiritual creature's irrational choice to turn away from the unchangeable good of union with God and to pursue the inconsistent and fragmentary goods of material reality. The illusion of evil can be corrected when the mind is illuminated by the true knowledge of the good.

Augustine's social concept of grace began to develop in his letter to Simplician (396 ce). Augustine interpreted Paul as teaching that, because all of humanity shares in Adam's sin, every return to God is the effect of God's prior grace. He also noted the importance of internal conflict in Romans 7, where the knowledge of the good does not result in the ability to do it, which led him to distinguish more sharply between the intellect and the will. During the twenty years of controversy with the Donatists and Pelagians that followed, Augustine recognized the importance of the will as the soul's social operation. He continued at this time to understand grace as persuasion and to protect the soul's self-determination in turning to God, but by 417 ce, Augustine repudiated this idea and embraced the absolute priority of the divine election.

He did so because he saw, through his reading of Origen, that the only way salvation could be secure was if it depended on God's act to produce the initial willing and perseverance in the elect. Once Augustine clearly differentiated the will from the intellect, and consequently grace from creation—in order to preserve the divine immutability that ensured the goodness of creation—God's will had to dominate the human will.

Aquinas would later resolve this predicament by joining his metaphysical actualism of Being to his more sophisticated understanding of the will, which resulted in a noncompetitive, social understanding of human self-determination. When the distinction between nature and the supernatural is understood in light of these concepts, the metaphysical bases for the unity of grace and creation are established by Catholic theology. But the social dimension of grace that Aquinas acknowledged with his appeal to charity and friendship could not be sustained in the absence of the critical concept that Luther later developed. Luther's doctrine of justification cast the theology of grace squarely in terms of a critical social relation that cut to the heart of scholasticism and the ecclesial society it reinforced. Luther's understanding of justification was based on the same actualist premises that informed Augustine's embrace of election and Aquinas's metaphysics of being. In the same way that Augustine recognized that Origenism could not ensure salvation, Luther argued that a justification that was contingent on an obligation to charity amounted to a truly impossible ethical ideal, a ruse of sinful self-preservation. But because Jesus is the form of faith, justification is the actuality of our reconciled relation with God, which is expressed in our faith. Because this unity with Christ is an ontological reality but lacks Aquinas's metaphysics of the will, human self-determination is merely a predicate of Christ's dominant subjectivity. Once again the social relation is lost, but in this case the absence is concealed within its explicitly social terms.

As I adumbrated at the close of chapter 3, a way beyond this deadlock passes through Aquinas's metaphysics of Being and the will combined with the Reformers' critical concept of grace as a social relation. In each of the failures I have analyzed, it is the inability to sustain a coherent metaphysics of social relations that creates these abstract formulas. In the remainder of my study, I will develop these resources to offer a programmatic sketch for the unity of grace and creation as an actually existing social relation.

CREATION: THE BEING OF THE OTHER

[T]he very precocious idea that certain formal notions are not fully intelligible except in a concrete event, which seems even more irrational than the notions, but through which they are truly thought.

—EMMANUEL LEVINAS

I have argued that the union of creation and grace as a social relation is the goal toward which these doctrines have been striving, even as this relation has been unknowingly but consistently elided. The root of that elision has been the inability to keep clear on the will's distinction from the intellect and desire. The four theologians I have investigated ran aground on what Hegel identified as the abstract form of thought in bourgeois social relations.[1] This is true even in contemporary Protestant theology, where the critical function of grace is conceived socially.

This abstractness is only strengthened by the failure fully to understand creation ex nihilo as the ontological constitution of a social relation. Resolving this difficulty requires that we now begin to understand creation as the voluntary, positive action to establish the being of the other. For this reason, the doctrine of creation is incomplete when it is conceived only in terms of ontological participation.[2] In creating, God not only brings into being that which is not Being itself but also establishes the creature as a being distinct from God, with its own operational integrity.[3] God creates a creature, a created participation in uncreated Being, but the essence of this being is to be an *other*. Its existence is a social relation.

Because creation founds a social relation, God's creating is an ethical action. Creation is good because God is present to it, but God is present because the world is the distinct object of the divine will. As the act of existence, God's social relation with creation is one of mutuality and harmony, not contrast and competition. Attempts to achieve this relation apart from the doctrine of creation ex nihilo, like Catherine Keller's in *Face of the Deep*, miss that it is the metaphysical asymmetry of the relation between the Creator and the creature that ensures the possibility of this relation.[4] To maintain, as she does, the notion that God and creation together subsist in an absolute relation is itself an ontological expression of the bourgeois subjectivity.[5]

God's relation to the creature is a positive determination of the creature as an other, in its otherness. God establishes the being of the other and affirms the other in its existence. Creation is the concupiscent object of God's activity of creating. When we think of creation in these social terms, we can speak of the creative act as charity. In Aquinas's terms, God takes the good of another as God's own. And it is this aspect of God's act that associates the goodness of creation directly with intersubjective relation. Established and affirmed as God's other, the natural operation of the self-determining will of the spiritual creature is not self-preservation. The desire expressed in the will's action is an innate yearning for its union with God. Prior to any drive to preserve itself in existence, the creature is summoned to imitate God in living for the other. Because its being is founded as the constitution of God's other, the yearning to live for the other also includes, derivatively, the desire to preserve oneself. But the nature of this existence, aspiring for the other, is that we affirm our lives only in living them for the other. Self-preservation is the primordial impulse to affirm the positivity of our own otherness. When this impulse miscarries and becomes a preoccupation with securing an identity in contrast to others, then this urge is sin.

The intellect's natural knowledge of the other is abstract. The will, however, is not. Even when willing the general, rather than special, good, the will is ordered to the material and historical. To will the good is to will it in reality, not ideality. And, unlike desire, the will does not, principally, seek to overcome privation and to satiate appetite. The drive to satisfy desire is fundamentally a positive affirmation of the goodness of its own otherness. Even in quenching its own desires, it is the material and historical other that the will wills, seeks, delights in, and enjoys. The will seeks to affirm in the individual the universal value, meaning, and significance of the otherness of material being.

The will is the self's capacity for the affirmation of the other. When it fails positively to affirm the other, when it reduces the other to the sameness of even immanent difference, the natural orientation of the will is disordered. By extension, the will's relation to God, creation, and the self is disordered as well. This claim reverses the ontological abstractness of the order of charity, because the height of the created experience of the good passes ineluctably through the material history of an other creature. As David Burrell has brilliantly observed, God's knowledge is convertible with God's will, which means that God knows creatures in the very practical act of creating them and in the immediacy of their material existence.[6] God knows creation as the other in creating it. Rightly knowing any being, therefore, includes the willing affirmation of the existence of the other. The perception of truth is uniquely bound to our positive willing of the reality of the other.

God's creating establishes a social existence; it founds existence as social. Our immediate intuition of existence is of this social relation, which includes recognition of the *absolute otherness* of the creator. Awareness of the absolute dependence of being is simultaneously the perception of the otherness of created being. Awareness of the otherness of created being is also the apprehension of the absolute other on whose act one's existence, value, meaning, and significance depend. The otherness of created being is the self-communication of Godself—the offer of communion—within created reality. The immediacy of this relation to existence also means, as Aquinas maintained, that the aim of this social existence is friendship with God.

Because the natural orientation of the will is for the positive affirmation of the existence of the other, the aim of the will is beyond its innate powers to produce. The obligation is not impossible, because this orientation to the other is the essential form of the will's operation. It depends not on the imposition of an ideal that lies infinitely beyond it capacities but on the reception of the actuality of the love of an other. The conditions for the perfection of the will's natural desire for the other depends upon the willing self-bestowal of a love that is distinct from itself. The will cannot produce, attain, or enjoy this love apart from the other. And our salvation depends on the reception of the prior actuality of the love of God. It is in this way that we can affirm the grace that fulfills nature.

GRACE: THE CRITICAL SOCIAL RELATION OF THE OTHER

Grace is God's fidelity to the being of the other whom God has created. In this fidelity, God's identity is bound to the existence of the other. In creating, God affirms, preserves, and sustains the existence of the other, but in bestowing grace God gives Godself to the other. This act of self-bestowal is also volitional, a decision to bind Godself to creation. In the act of creation, God assumes the good of the other as God's own. In conferring grace, God's distinctiveness is bound up with this relation. It is in this regard that election is significant, specifically as the decision to set apart a particular people as a blessing to all. Grace is the continual affirmation of the being of the other within the context of the social relation established by creation.

This fidelity creates new possibilities for created being. As Oliva Blanchette noted of Aquinas, multiplicity is central to created perfection, because the greater risks that come with complexity also increase the possibility for expressing the good. As a result, willing the good of individual beings does not preserve the transcendental order of the same (for example, the *ordo caritas*) but risks disorder for the sake of creating new possibilities for realizing communion, especially between heaven and earth. That communion is not a fact of creation but the task of grace. It is accomplished by the grace through which God continually binds Godself to the being of the other in its creation. This grace perfectly coincides with and even extends the act of creating, but because it incorporates and includes the relation and response of the other, it is distinct from it.

The possibility of grace and its reception is established in creation, but the realization of the social relation transforms existence. This recognition of the ontological transformation of the realization of the good should be the way in which to appeal to the Neoplatonic category of the "beyond" or the "above being." The goodness of created existence is not a transcendental ideal above existence, "beyond being," as in Levinas, nor the merely socially constructive "good that is also nothing" of Deleuze.[7] The grace that perfects creation is that which is only anticipated by created being now as the good that is *not-yet*, the charitable differentiation of existence that is not yet completed.[8] It is the event in the social life of existence in which the creature's self-determination is most transparent to the benevolence of its Origin, the act of the Creator. Because creation is a social relation, new and unanticipated harmonious social relations are true expressions of divine creativity.

The act of charity that fulfills the natural impulse of the will is always the realization of a new dimension of created being. Grace is God's continued fidelity to the being of the other, through which new social configurations of the unity of existence emerge, and through which acts of charity continue to remain possible for humanity. In creating, God assumes the good of the existence of the other as God's own, but by grace the creature assumes that same good as its own. This is the paradox of the social understanding of the unity of grace and creation. Complete human happiness consists in an act of self-bestowing love that is completely coincident with its object. Because its object is God's absolute affirmation of created otherness, its object includes itself. Only an act that is completely transparent to God's absolute affirmation of the being of the other can fulfill the natural orientation of the will's operation. Luther liked to highlight the critical social dimension of Christ's work that is *pro me*, and because that work is for me, God is revealed to be *pro nobis*, for us. But in the current frame, when this insight is explicitly linked with Aquinas's metaphysics of the act of existence, we can say that God's grace is united with God's creating in the fact that is always *pro te*, for you.[9]

Justification is the actuality of this grace as a social relation. It precedes, determines, and makes possible our acts of cooperation. Faith is the expression of the reality of that relation in us, our own participation in God's fidelity to the being of the other. It is in this way that God's act becomes ours. But the act that is ours, in this case, is the same one that gives us being, gives us to ourselves, enables us to act, and directs us to the other. Right as Luther was in his diagnosis of self-preservation as a failure of the will, that drive is not the problem to overcome. Rather, what we must learn to affirm about ourselves, in knowledge and in act, is that our lives come into being as given to the other. Self-bestowal is not abnegation but fulfillment. Because we exist in God's eternal ethical act, which is aimed at the realization of our harmonious mutuality, all of being is oriented to the perfection of the enjoyment of the existence of the other.

Created existence is a relation between God and the creature who exists. What happens between them occurs on the basis of God's fidelity to the being of the other and cannot be accounted for simply in terms of the present coordinates of existence. New aspects of being emerge because of the ethical relation between God and creatures, which includes the relation between creatures themselves. Because our faith expresses the actuality of God's fidelity to the being of the other, our own faith is a participation in God's act of creating.

JESUS CHRIST: MEDIATOR OF THE OTHER

Because the path to God moves through the positive affirmation of the being of the other, it is fitting that our justification occurs through the faith of the individual Jesus of Nazareth. God appears in material history in the life of our neighbor Jesus Christ. The relation of every individual to him is entirely unique, because he is at once wholly divine (absolute and universal) and wholly human (relative and individual).

Only in Jesus Christ is our created otherness revealed in immediate coincidence with God's absolute otherness. This coincidence means that the affirmation of the goodness and meaning of the creation are inseparable from the affirmation of the "unsubstitutability" of the otherness of this man.[10] Hans Frei claimed in *The Identity of Jesus Christ* that the gospel's witness to Jesus's identity as the crucified and resurrected Christ perfectly coincides with the experience of his presence. In the gospel's narrating who Jesus was, the audience's recognition of the coherence of the narrative—the acknowledgment of the truth of its identification of him—immediately corresponds to an encounter with Jesus himself, as the Living One.[11] The Gospels recognize no hiatus in the meaning of the narrative and actuality of his resurrection. Not to accede to the truth of the narrative is to deny its coherence and to claim a different identity for Jesus—that he is not alive with God's life. But if the coherence of the narrative is accepted and he is recognized as the resurrected Christ, then this has happened by the power of his resurrection.

This insight can illuminate the place of Jesus Christ as the Mediator in my reconstruction of the unity of grace and creation. The Gospels' presentation of the identity of Jesus of Nazareth as the resurrected Lord is a directive to acknowledge his irreducible, unsubstitutable uniqueness. The Gospels are an announcement of his absolute distinctiveness, a call to recognize his inimitable difference. If God has acted to raise this man from the dead, then this single human being is of eternal significance for all. To affirm the eternal significance of his life is to locate the meaning of historical material life in relation to him. If he is not unique among human beings, then he is just like all others in that he will one day no longer be known, his identity dominated by death. If this is the truth of existence, then distinctive differentiation is also a pure illusion. Any meaningful identity, any otherness at all, is merely abstract and negative, an expression of the more impulsive power of self-preservation. But if he is the resurrected One, then it is in relation to him alone that any individual existence has meaning and significance as an other. Because this one individual is God's elect, the eternal significance of every other is secured in relation to him. He is eternally significant to each one, and the significance of every other lies in the status of its relation to him.

Affirmation of Christ's unique significance for every other is simultaneously the recognition of his divinity. The otherness of the individual human being Jesus of Nazareth is unsubstitutable because it is absolute. His universal significance is not a generality. Because God has raised this man from the dead, it is the identity of this specific man that has universal significance to the existence of every other being. To say that his otherness, his identity, is absolute is to say that it does not persist in contrast to any other identity. It is not abstractly or negatively constructed. He is not himself because of an exclusion of any other. His unique identity is, rather, the condition of possibility for the recognition of the eternal significance of any other at all. He is what delivers us from the self-preserving drive to construct ourselves in opposition to one another. His identity is the universal positivity of every identity.

In being determined by his unsubstitutable identity, our selves are not predicates of his absolute subjectivity. We become most fully ourselves as we learn to affirm the truth revealed in his creative fidelity to us. To participate in that act, by the Spirit, through our faith, is to be drawn into the eternal relation of the Son to the Father, the unending "begottenness" of the Word.[12] This act of divinization is possible only because of the actuality of God's grace in Christ. The act by which we are to give ourselves away to God and to another occurs only in Christ. His oblation of himself to God is inseparable from the gift of himself to us. The act in which he gives himself away coincides immediately with the act by which God bears us into existence. Teresa of Avila was keen to remind us that the deeper we move into our own souls, the more significant it is to discover that it is Jesus himself whom we find there.[13] In very different language, Frei said the same thing when he remarked that "when God speaks, Jesus appears." This is a true deification. Our union with Jesus is our union with God. Unity with God transforms our acts into participations in God's act of creating. The grace of divine fidelity expressed in our faith is the instrument of God's continued creativity. What God creates, through Christ, is a material and social relation.

ATTENDANCE: THINKING THE UNITY OF CREATION AND GRACE

> *This authentically human factor is passion, in which the one generation also fully understands the other and understands itself. Thus no generation has learned from another how to love, no generation can begin other than at the beginning, the task of no later generation is shorter than its predecessor's, and if someone unlike the previous generation, is unwilling to stay with love but wants to go further, then that is simply idle and foolish talk.*
>
> —SØREN KIERKEGAARD, *FEAR AND TREMBLING*

The unity with Christ is not ideal or merely noetic. Protestant theology was right to challenge the metaphysical immediacy of the Catholic model of nature and the supernatural in the name of grace as a critical concept of social relations. Yet, Protestantism's separation from metaphysics resulted in the reduction of the social dimension of its critical concept to an abstract and negative principle.

In this light, we must now recognize that the union of grace with creation is, specifically, a critical social relation. It is not in any simplistic sense the perpetual disruption of so-called natural metaphysical stability, and it is not the invocation of the normative but impossible ideal for social life. It is the actual social expression of the unity of God and creation, which is the material history of the positive affirmation of the existence of the other.

It is on this point that I run up against the limits of this discourse. The horizon of thought that I am rapidly approaching is not the sublime, the gap between our sensory imagination and the reality we encounter. It is the horizon on which the talk of a critical social relation subtly shifts to an ideal surrogate for reality, a substitute for an actually existing social relation. Here is the moment in this discursive study when the determination of my thought by the prior abstract illusions of bourgeois social forms may be repeated and reinforced just when I experience the attempt to resolve those illusions. Here is the point when Derrida would insist on leaving the wound of discourse exposed to the undecidable. The very momentum of my analysis, to say nothing of the social pressures of academic theology, surges toward the imposition of the concept that will reconcile these doctrines. But at the same moment, the desire expressed in my study rushes forward to the affirmation of the other, away from the abstract and toward the material and the social. I must name the impulse to abstractness, and in naming it begin to speak within the pressures to leave history with new forms of thought more adequate to the actual realities communicated in the doctrines of creation and grace.

The lure is to appeal to the other as a regulative ideal, imposed on the necessarily unjust social relations of existence—what Levinas calls "ontology." Yet Terry Eagleton is certainly right—and Gillian Rose before him—to say that that sort of ethical demand participates in and supports the violent illusions it so furiously mourns.[14] Another lure, which has gained traction in recent theology, seeks an alternative to this social fragmentation in the immediate metaphysics of the intuitive unity of the other with reality, calling this the unity of grace with creation.[15] But this, too, would subsume grace to creation and obviate the social relation actualized by the act of creating. Instead of this impulse to uncover unity in identity, we must allow the immediate experience of social reality to reconfigure the significance of the critical concept of grace. We must conceive the unity of grace and creation as a summons to a specific social unity. This summons is not a call to think the reality of a social relation creatively, in terms that do not now exist; it is a call to think from the actuality of the social conditions of charity.

Because this relation is an actuality, we must think its reality in spite of the risks. The reality is inseparable from the risk. Gillian Rose proposed that we always think from the "broken middle" in order not to evade the risks of thinking the absolute in history.[16] Yet, although I certainly think her analysis is right, Christian theology knows the world's determination by the self-communication of the agent of creation in the grace of Jesus of Nazareth. Christian theology is obliged to say more than the righteous agnosticism of the "broken middle" can sustain. Nonetheless, taking Rose seriously means that we will have to think about the responsibility of thought in the midst of this social fragmentation. We are obliged to think the metaphysical reality of Being as a social relation.

Though Simone Weil often tended toward a Manichaean metaphysics of the material world, it is she above others who highlighted the ethical, social responsibility of thought. She described the right relation of the abstract mind's relation to concrete history as one of *attendance*, waiting.[17] In one of her more significant reflections on this waiting, "Reflections on the Right Use of School Studies with a View to the Love of God," Weil wrote:

> Attention consists of suspending our thought, leaving it detached, empty, and ready to be penetrated by the object; it means holding in our minds, within reach of this thought, but on a lower level and not in contact with it, the diverse knowledge we have acquired which we are forced to make use of. Our thought should be in relation to all particular and already formulated thoughts, as a man on a mountain who, as he looks forward, sees also below him, without actually looking at them, a great many forests and plains. Above all our thought should be empty, waiting, not seeking anything, but ready to receive in its naked truth the object that is to penetrate it.[18]

The mind is naturally waiting on the world. All the truth the mind knows, it has perceived because of prayer. In learning a new language or understanding geometry, the knowledge that is attained eventually becomes transparent to its object by abandoning itself in an affirmation of its reality. In this abandonment, the mind is not passive, because it is realizing the truth of its ethical relation to reality. The mind is obliged to be actively attuned to the self-expression of creation, to *wait* upon it. The mind comes to know, in its activity, that its efforts to apprehend the object only hinder knowing it, that truth includes the affirmation of the existence of the otherness of the object.[19] Theology must cultivate the practice of this attentive, contemplative awareness in thinking.[20]

The mind's immediate intuition of itself in its absolute dependence is awareness of its status as an other. The immediate spontaneity of the self arises within the primal sociality of the origin of the self. The self is not the universal exception to reality in its capacity for spontaneity; it is the positive constitution of an irreducible relation of dependence on God, summoned to the possibility of eternal communion with God. Knowledge of this immediate awareness of the self in this relation is, therefore, apophatic. It marks an originary perception of the plentitude of God's superlative, positive determination of one's being in its otherness. This otherness always subsists in excess of the abstract "sameness" through which the mind knows that other in its manifestation.

But *attendance* is not only waiting in anticipation and awareness, it is also waiting as tending, serving, nurturing, cultivating. In anticipative awareness of being, attendance is active care for the existence of the other. Waiting in this sense is a response to the bidding of being, which gives itself to us in giving us to one another and, through one another, to ourselves. Waiting is our active response to the intrinsically ethical sociality of being. Waiting is our fidelity to the being of the other, our intentional cooperation with the act of existence (*ipsum esse*). Waiting is the obligation to service. The apophatic immediacy of our relation to God's creativity is conceptually determined in dialogue, which is the affirmation of the ineluctable social determination of thought. It is in dialogue that the critical conceptual work is undertaken to submit our metaphysical intuition to scrutiny for justification while the social nature of our being is attended to.

Two conclusions follow from this way of framing the relationship of waiting to our being. First, this notion of waiting links ontology to social reality in a radically nondual way. David Burrell often points positively to the work of Sara Grant, who affirms that Aquinas's metaphysics is a nondualism.[21] I have sought here to move beyond the intellectualist frame within which this nondualism is expressed and to highlight its explicitly volitional, ethical, and social aspects. These are the dimensions of creation ex nihilo that are rarely affirmed but which my study has shown to be of integral metaphysical significance to it.

Second, this nondual social relation finally resolves the fundamental tension between the Augustinian-Lombardian-Lutheran position that charity simply is the presence of the grace of the Holy Spirit, and Aquinas's keen insight that the act of charity must be our own. If we understand creation as the constitution of the being of the other and grace as the sustained fidelity to it, then God's presence immediately facilitates my own self-determination. My capacity for self-determination is the immediate result of my being as God's creature, which orders my life to the positive affirmation of the otherness of created existence. But my capacity for charity, which fulfills that goal, is made possible by my determination by a justified social relation with God and others. The appearance of this social relation is a genuine transformation of created existence. That social relation expresses God's new relation to creation in Christ. In that relation, the world is rendered transparent to God's creative act through its own active participation in it. This participation is its deification, which is the irreducible social and material form in which grace and creation are unified.

This social relation is the rule of God, God's dominion. Where God rules, there is unity in freedom. Importantly, the church is not this social relation. As *Lumen Gentium* states, "The Church is in Christ like a sacrament or as a sign and instrument both of a very closely knit union with God and of the unity of the whole human race."[22] The church is the sign and instrument of the unity of humanity, but it is not the reality of that unity.[23] The church participates in God's reign and is now a sacrament of it. Like our faith, it is the expression of the actuality of God's dominion, but it is not its realization. The church serves the kingdom: it looks in anticipation for its being, seeks an awareness of its presence, serves its flourishing, and waits for its completion. In each of these ways, the church recognizes that it is co-missioned by Christ to live its life as the expression of God's fidelity to the existence of the other.

The most urgent task confronting the social reality of the church at present is to live into the reality of a social relation beyond the bourgeois opposition of the subject and nature, the individual and the universal. Taking that task seriously, which means moving decisively beyond abstract and negative surrogates for the true historical and material work of love, will compel the church out of the enclaves, out of the culture wars, out of the fetishizing of the margins and its opposition to "culture" and "the world," in whatever form these illusions take. It will compel the church to live concretely beyond the fantasized performances of the abstractly and negatively determined "identities" that divide us from one another. It will force us to disclaim as self-serving the idea of a church whose witness is not physically invested in and devoted to the civic, legal, and political well-being of the social relations that sustain it. And it will do so by expressing the actuality of God's charity in the material life of a specific place. The union of grace with creation is a church that lives to express in the world the flourishing of life that God desires for all. It will create and support transformative and life-giving innovations in how we produce and distribute food, how we labor, how we care for children, how we care for our cities, and how we heal the sick and collectively meet our obligation to them. It will mean not simply living with and caring for the poor, but the unequivocal dedication to the eradication of the conditions that create and sustain the social reality of poverty. Our difficulty, the church's difficulty, in not just doing these things but to understand them as the expression of the actuality of redemption, as the site of the union of grace and creation. Doing so will require courageous confrontation with the central social illusion, the hidden engine of our life together—that illusion that is the duty of the catholic church in our time to expose and confound: the bourgeois self.

We are not, by nature, creators. We are creatures. But because creation itself is a social reality, it is in our life together that we receive the grace, with God, to create. God's new act includes us and is made with us. This grace is the fulfillment of the act of creation.

Notes

1. See Gillian Rose, *Hegel contra Sociology* (New York: Verso, 2009), 51–97.

2. For a nuanced acceptance of the emanationist position, see David Burrell, "Creation or Emanation: Two Paradigms of Reason," in *God and Creation*, ed. Bernard McGinn and David Burrell (Notre Dame, IN: University of Notre Dame Press, 1990).

3. See Thomas Aquinas, *Summa theologiae* 1.45.1. Compare this notion of operational integrity with Levinas's idea of "originary substitution" in Emmanuel Levinas, *Otherwise Than Being; or, Beyond Essence*, trans. Alphonso Lingis (Pittsburgh: Duquesne University Press, 1998), 99–129.

4. See Catherine Keller, *Face of the Deep: A Theology of Becoming* (New York: Routledge, 2003).

5. Catherine Keller, In the Face of the Deep: A Theology of Becoming (New York: Routledge, 2003).

6. David Burrell makes this claim in numerous places, but it is more characteristic of his early work, where he emphasizes a distinctly practical knowledge in God's works. See Burrell, "Creation or Emanation"; Burrell, "Divine Practical Knowing: How an Eternal God Acts in Time," in *Divine Action*, ed. Brian Hebblethwaite and Edward Henderson (Edinburgh: T & T Clark, 1990); and Burrell, *Aquinas, God, and Action* (Notre Dame, IN: University of Notre Dame Press, 1979). Burrell's most recent work explicitly notes that his view of freedom implies that knowledge of the good implies the capacity to perform it. See *Faith and Freedom: An Interfaith Perspective*, Challenges in Contemporary Theology (Malden, MA: Blackwell, 2004). This strikes me as an unusual and unnecessary claim. This development appears to coincide with Burrell's greater appreciation for the Platonic tradition in general, especially emanationism. See Burrell, "Creation or Emanation."

7. In his lectures "On Spinoza," Deleuze notes: "In a pure Ontology, where there is no One superior to being, I say evil is nothing, there is no evil, there is being. Okay. But that engages me with something completely new[;] it is that if evil is nothing, then the good is nothing either. It is thus for completely opposite reasons that I can say in both cases that evil is nothing. In one case, I say that evil is nothing because only the Good makes being and makes action[;] in the other case, I say that evil is nothing because the Good is nothing too, because there is only being. Now we have seen that this negation of the good, like that of evil, did not prevent Spinoza from making an ethics. How is an ethics made if there is neither good nor evil[?] From the same formula, in the same era, if you take the formula: [evil] is nothing, signed by Leibniz, and signed by Spinoza, they

both say the same formula, [evil] is nothing, but it has two opposite senses. In Leibniz it derives from Plato, and in Spinoza, who makes a pure ontology, it becomes complicated." This section is a response to a question prompted by the transcription of the lecture at "Lectures by Gilles Deleuze," online at http://deleuzelectures.blogspot.com/2007/02/on-spinoza.html.

8. This way of phrasing the matter is inspired by John Westerhoff's lecture "The Priest as Catechist," on the cassette recording *The Priest as a Spiritual Resource*, Episcopal Radio-TV Foundation, Atlanta, 1985.

9. Hans Urs von Balthasar makes a similar claim in *Mysterium Paschale: The Mystery of Easter*, trans. Aidan Nichols (San Francisco: Ignatius Press, 2000), 139.

10. Hans Frei, *The Identity of Jesus Christ* (Eugene, OR: Wipf & Stock, 1997), 91 and 104.

11. Ibid., 186–95.

12. See Sarah Coakley, "Why Three? Some Further Reflections on the Origins of the Doctrine of the Trinity," in *The Making and Remaking of Christian Doctrine: Essays in Honour of Maurice Wiles*, eds. Sarah Coakley and David Pailin (Oxford: Clarendon Press, 1993), 29–56; and Mark McIntosh, *Divine Teaching: An Introduction to Christian Theology* (Malden, MA: Blackwell, 2008), 111–38.

13. Teresa of Avila, *The Interior Castle* 22.2 (New York: Paulist, 1979), 11. See Rowan Williams, *Teresa of Avila* (Harrisburg, PA: Morehouse, 1991), 90–91. The same impulse resides in the *hesychasts* as well, in their prayer "Jesus Christ, Son of God, have mercy on me, a sinner." See the interesting essay by George Lindbeck titled "Hesychastic Prayer and the Christianizing of Platonism: Some Protestant Reflections," in *The Church in a Postliberal Age* (Grand Rapids, MI: Eerdmans, 2002), 106–19.

14. See Terry Eagleton, *The Trouble with Strangers: A Study of Ethics* (Malden, MA: Blackwell, 2008); and Gillian Rose, *Mourning Becomes the Law: Philosophy and Representation* (Cambridge: Cambridge University Press, 1996), as represntative examples.

15. Examples abound and are too numerous to list. They are, however, generally invested heavily, in Catholic circles, in the theology of Henri de Lubac and Hans Urs von Balthasar, and, in Protestant circles, in the work of George Lindbeck and Hans Frei. This is a trajectory that is invested in specific intepretations of these figures that seek to distinguish them from modernity, subjectivity, and liberalism (political and theological). A small but growing contingency of theologians is, in the anxiety evoked by any appeal to subjectivity at all, returning to arguments for the neo-scholastic objectivity of grace. See Reinhard Hütter, *Dust Bound for Heaven: Explorations in the Theology of Thomas Aquinas* (Grand Rapids, MI: Eerdmans, 2012); Steven A. Long, *Natura Pura: On the Recovery of Nature in the Doctrine of Grace* (New York: Fordham University Press, 2010); and Lawrence Feingold, *The Natural Desire to See God according to St. Thomas and His Interpreters* (Ave Maria, FL: Sapientia Press of Ave Maria University, 2010).

16. Gillian Rose, *The Broken Middle: Out of Our Ancient Society* (Malden, MA: Blackwell, 1992).

17. See the discussions of the significance of "attention" in Janet Sockice, *The Kindness of God* (Oxford: Oxford University Press, 2007), 7–34; and Iris Murdoch, *The Sovereignty of the Good* (New York: Routledge, 2002), 1–44.

18. Simone Weil, *Waiting for God*, trans. Emma Craufurd (New York: Harper, 2009), 62.

19. See ibid., 105–16.

20. Though the mind is immediately ordered to the other by its being, it must learn a facility in attentive thinking, through spiritual practice. Sarah Coakley has emphasized this more than any other contemporary systematic theologian.

21. Sara Grant, *Towards an Alternative Theology: Confessions of a Non-Dualist Christian* (Notre Dame, IN: University of Notre Dame Press, 2001).

22. The quotation is from the Vatican II document *Lumen Gentium*, §1.

23. On the passing away of the church in the eschaton, see Herbert McCabe, "Christ and Politics," in *God Still Matters* (New York: Continuum, 2002), 79–91.

Index

Additional Praise

"Davis's book reveals a deep thinker in close conversation with the richest sources of our contemporary theological tradition, one who creatively challenges longstanding dividing lines between nature and grace, Protestant and Catholic. This dense and demanding essay will not just invite re-reading; it will also repay the effort."

Paul J. DeHart
Vanderbilt University

"A learned, far-reaching, and valuable book. Joshua Davis's complex and provocative argument—which engages authors ranging from Augustine to Gillian Rose, and culminates in a striking constructive statement—opens up important new lines of thought and deserves close attention."

Paul Dafydd Jones
University of Virginia

CPSIA information can be obtained at www.ICGtesting.com
Printed in the USA
LVOW13s1220120913

352155LV00003B/6/P